If You Can Make It Through The Night

Acknowledgments

First, I would like to thank Big Papa (God). I am and never have been anything without him. I am thankful for his grace and mercy. To my son, Adam, thank you for reviving my heart, showing me how to love unconditionally, teaching me patience, strength, and persistence. My dear boy you saved me. To my grandparents, Erma Burris and Tony Kirkwood. I have no words to express the magnitude of my gratitude. Granny you were the sun and grandpa and you were the moon. To my mother, thank you for teaching me resilience, confidence, and pride.

To my dear friend, Jalica Davis-Stewart, I completed this book on the anniversary of your death. We had a conversation months before your death about both of us finishing our projects, we were excited. We said that we couldn't wait to read what the other had written. I'll never get to read your book. Your unexpected death reminded me that we are on borrowed time and the time to live is now! Thank you for giving me the push to complete this book. It took five years, but I finally did it.

To my All-Star Team Cieaira Tucker, Crystal Gordon, Marshell Lane, Rachel Williams, Ambria Webb, Lenita Tidwell, Shamika Allen, Queen Nzingha Olakanwa, Lashonda Horton-Polain, Geralyn Grice, Torre Wright, Clinton Snelling, Tony Scott, Dr. Willie Ann Hart, Tyrone Bailey, George

Kirkwood, Joe Kirkwood, Freddy Kirkwood, Bobby Kirkwood, Isaac Huddleston, Michael Simelton, Donnie McClinton Jr, Byron Brown, all of my cousins, aunts, and uncles, Thank you! every one of you has played a significant role in my life in some shape, form, or fashion. Thank you for being the stars in my Solar System. You all have motivated, supported, criticized, had my back even when you were not aware of it. Thank you for being my village.! To professor Corey Hall Thank you for sparking the flame that ignited this process. Thank you for your listening ear and wealth of editorial expertise during this process. Thank you for pushing me to be a better a writer.

I do not have to sell a million copies or become a best-selling author. I only want to encourage, inspire, motivate and ignite something in someone. This is a story to let someone know that no matter what you go through, what choices you make, or what cards you are dealt, you can make it! If you make it through that night, you can make it! It's not over or all lost. Every day is a new day to change the world, reinvent yourself, elevate! We die once, but we live every day. Make your day count.

Chapters

I. Dear Mama
II. Starring Through My Rearview
III. Running Dying To Live
IV. Guess Who's Back?
V. Shit Don't Stop
VI. This Aint living
VII. Ambitions AZ A Ridah
VIII. Got My Mind Made Up
IX. Changes
X. Trading War Stories
XI. Keep Ya Head Up
XII. Me against the World
XIII. Play Your Cards Right
XIV. Troublesome
XV. Death Around the Corner
XVI. Shorty Wanna Be a Thug
XVII. Toss It Up
XVIII. Thug Passion
XIX. A Letter to My Unborn Child pg.
XX. Shed So Many Tears
XXI. Only God Can Judge Me

Prologue

I was birthed by a fourteen-year-old child, have never met my father, and never kept the same address for more than a year. I'm supposed to be a statistic. Data show that I should be dead, in jail, or following in my mother's footsteps with a house full of children. Sometimes the numbers point to fact, and sometimes they don't. My childhood was far from the best. I read my first novel in the first grade. It was a Herculean romance novel that I had stolen from my aunt. I remember my teacher discovering me reading the novel. I tried to pretend I didn't know how to read it, but she knew that I did. She made such a big deal about it, and I couldn't understand why. A first grader reading a Herculean romance novel didn't seem unusual for me.

I didn't realize it then, but reading a lot was the greatest thing that I did for myself. Reading helped me in school and, it also helped me in life. I learned logic and reasoning skills from reading. I gained critical-thinking skills, and a large vocabulary. I probably have read over a million books in my lifetime. I always say I'm going to get all my library cards from every school or public library that I checked books from, but that still wouldn't account for even half of the books I have read. I would always read a book and imagine my own words on the page, imagining how I would have written it or how I would tell my story.

I always would go back and forth with a book's beginning and ending. I believe book should always begin with a life- changing event and end with a life- changing event, for the beginning of this book, I chose an event that was life changing for me. I have had many of things happen that could be considered life-changing, but this one stuck the most. This book begins with a realization and the first of many adult decisions, rational or irrational.

I wrote this book to tell my story about beating the odds. People I'm living proof that all things are possible. It just takes hard work and sacrifice, and, sometimes doing what you do not want to do to get what you want. I wasn't given anything in life. I worked for everything I have and learned from everything I lost. The chapters being named after Tupac Shakur Song's, are because, through all those crazy days and nights, his music saved me. Tupac's music allowed me to vent and express myself. I remember shutting my door, turning on Tupac and just zoning out.

Tupac kept me sane; his music was my outlet. I could relate to everything Tupac rapped about, and I wasn't even an adult yet. I have experienced homelessness, being fatherless, feeling misunderstood, racism, sexism, and loneliness. I first heard Tupac when I was in the third grade and never stopped listening. Tupac died when I was in the fifth grade, whenever I was living with my grandmother. I remember watching the news whenever something about Tupac came on, then finally they announced he was dead and me and my grandma both cried like he was a relative. I knew the world had lost someone special, a man before his time, a man that could entice a crowd with songs like "Hit 'em up" and bring them to tears with songs like "Dear Mama" or "Keep Ya Head Up." *"If you can make it through the night there is a brighter day, everything will be alright if you hold on"*

Dear Mama

It was my junior year; I was working at McDonald's and my mother and I were living in a hotel. It wasn't the first time that we lived in a hotel; we had stayed in hotels before, but never for a long period of time. I was in the room reading a book, waiting on my mom to return. I heard a knock at the door. I went to the door, looked out the peep hole and saw the hotel manager's daughter. "Yes?" I said, "Is your mom here?" she asked I answered no; she said, "well I need you guys to pay the bill or move your things out" she said and then stomped off. I called my mom's cell phone to let her know what happened. My mom came back, and we went to the manager's office. My mom and the manager had a screaming match. I knew this wasn't a good thing, soon enough the manager was screaming at us to get out and to never come back. I had never felt so belittled and embarrassed in my life. The Salvation Army was paying for us to stay there, and we had maxed out our days. We either had to pay our own money or get out. I look back now and realize our days had been maxed out, because my cousin, Inez saw my mom at the Salvation Army trying to get us more stays, and she had given my mom money.

I think that was the only help my mom accepted during that time. I remember offering to pay for our stay with my McDonald's money, but my mom never accepted it. She wanted me to keep my money for my cell phone, lunch money, and other necessities, so we packed all our things, got in the car and drove away. I could see on my mom's face that this was the breaking point. We had nowhere to go. In all actuality we had plenty of places to go, but because my mom was so prideful, none of those places were options. As we drove, I kept thinking to myself, "How do we keep ending up in situations like this? Why won't anybody help us?" And ironically enough will I have to call off work tomorrow? See, even though we were living in a hotel, I was still going to school and working. I was always on time, never called off, and dedicated to my job. I took it seriously even though I was only making $5.25 an hour. I was grateful for my job. It paid for my cell phone, clothes, even u-hauls and furniture for us at times. I wasn't working because I wanted to; I had to work.

    My mom wasn't keeping work regularly. She couldn't meet all my needs, even my basic needs. I couldn't wait to go get a worker's permit at fifteen and a half so I could take matters into my own hands. By making my own money, I would also have to pick up slack at home. I cannot count how many U-hauls and electricity bills that I paid. I used to laugh at people that said, "Girl your mama keep you dressed" If they only knew. My mom did have some good luck times and when she had the money, I could get what I wanted from her. It just seems like the older I got, the worse things at home became. Maybe they were already bad, and I was just too young to realize. I remember having it good at times, and I remember having it bad. When I was five, I saw my mom be abused. At the age of eight I saw her get treated like a queen.

My earliest memories are about my mom and her chaotic relationship. The such relationship had an everlasting effect on me. I remember when we stayed in Illinois, that my mom met a guy from Detroit. The guy, Ray had a daughter. His daughter and I got along fine. My mom even used to dress us alike. Everything was fine until my mom found out Ray had been cheating on her with her cousin. My mom had it out with her cousin several times, but she never left Ray. My mom and Ray continued to argue and date, and then Ray's true colors started showing. I remember two incidents.

When my mother and I had come home one night from visiting one of her friends. She went to the refrigerator and poured us some water. I don't know if it was the smell or what, but before I could take a sip, she knocked the glass out my hand. She told me to go get my aunt. I ran to my aunt's house and told her what happened. She came to our house and called the paramedics. I remember them telling my mom to drink a lot of milk. I didn't know what was going on. We soon found out that Ray had broken into our home and put bleach in our drinking water. My mom had ingested some of the bleach before she smelled it. She didn't drink a lot, so she didn't have any major complications. Sadly, this still wasn't enough for her to leave Ray alone. My family started hating him. The town started hating him, and I started to hate him. It seemed like every day I was on edge, expecting something to happen. I was only five years old and feared men, all men.

It wasn't long before something else major happened. One night we were coming home, when we got to our doorstep, and Ray came up on the side of the porch and slammed my mom's head against the concrete wall. She passed out instantly. Again, I ran to my aunt's house. My mom was rushed to the hospital; she had suffered a major head injury. By this time everybody was fed up. Nobody was, going to let my mom go back to Ray. My mom eventually was released from the hospital and it was decided by some friends of hers, that something had to be done about Ray. It was clear that no matter how many times she left him; he would always find a way back. He would break in or sneak around outside on the regular. It was clear that the only way to get rid of Ray was to move out of town. My family and a few other guys from the projects we lived in then formed a plan. We had some cousins in Missouri, and they convinced my mom to move there. My family and a few guys from the projects packed all our stuff in a U-Haul. We were all set to leave, but not before Ray was handled.

We knew that once Ray heard about us leaving, he would and try to prevent it. Just like clockwork, the night before we left, Ray showed up. He and my mom argued through the window for a while. I remember my mama saying something about Ray's dead mother, and that was enough to cause him to react. Ray got so mad that he kicked the door in and ran up the steps. He didn't make it up three steps before twenty plus guys were on him. Ray thought that my mom was alone. He didn't know that she had all those guys waiting for him to do exactly what he did to her, Ray was beaten to a pulp. I remember hearing my mom screaming, because she thought they were going to kill him. I just stood there, dazed looking at all the blood everywhere I remember the floor being covered with blood. They beat Ray and then left him by the mailboxes. The apartment was eventually cleaned up, and we headed to Missouri. I remember looking at the trail of blood on the concrete as we drove away.

A few days later my grandmother called my mom telling her what was left of Ray. She said he was in the hospital barely holding on. Nobody knew what happened but the people in the house that night, and it stayed that way for a long time. My mom was so afraid she would go to jail, she didn't return to Illinois for a long time, and that is how we came to move to Missouri. We only moved forty-five minutes away, but it seemed like we moved much further. I started to hate men after seeing my mom go through those things with Ray. I thought they all were like Ray, and I expected all of them to turn out like him. I promised myself that, when I got older, I would kill Ray. I thought about how I would do it, but I changed the plan every year. I didn't see Ray again for years. I did see Ray when I was older, and he thought I would be happy to see him. I guess he didn't think a five-year-old could remember much. I told him to never speak or come near me again.

We moved to Missouri, but my mother's choice of men did not improve. She had several more abusive relationships. She even married an accused child molester. I used to stay up all night listening to them arguing so I could go upstairs and make myself known so he wouldn't hit her. Most of the time it worked, but sometimes it didn't. I trained myself to be a light sleeper, and I still am to this day. I can hear water running and wake up. People talking while I'm sleeping affects to the point that no one understands. She would argue and fight with this husband, and then he would put us out. We would be walking down the street in the middle of the night with our clothes. Sometimes we had our own house to go to and sometimes we had to go to someone else's house. I could not understand why she kept going back. To this day, she said it was because of his eight children. She loved his children and took care of them like her own.

I got short-changed because she treated me poorly just to make sure the other children didn't feel like she showed any favoritism towards me. However, I found a way out of that situation quickly. I left to stay with my aunt in Illinois. Staying with my aunt was the best thing that ever happened to me. She was my savior at the time. I was only in the third grade when I made this decision. My aunt took good care of me, taught me things, and I didn't have to be nervous waiting on the next time we were told to get out. I went back and forth between Illinois and Missouri from third through fifth grade. I got away, but my mother did not, until a few years later.

We didn't see any family for a very long time when we first moved to Missouri. I was enrolled in a predominately white school, which was much different from my previous school. We didn't know anyone but the cousins that stayed next door. I used to think about when and if I would ever see my grandmother, aunts, and cousins again. We didn't see any of our family when we first moved to Missouri. I used to think it was because my mother was scared that someone would find out she set Ray up or that she was scared she would run into him. I also thought maybe she was mad at our family, because that always seemed to be an issue. It seemed like someone in the family was always making her mad, judging her, or saying something about her.

My mother felt like the black sheep, and she still does today. As an adult, I have found out a lot about the reasons behind my mother's anger, and I do not I blame her. I also think that you shouldn't let the past dictate the person you are today. You must let it go and live your life to its maximum potential. My mother never learned to do that, so she walks around with emotions from the past built, and she explodes periodically. I try to live my life in the present, not in the past. I do not place blame on anyone for anything. I could blame my mom for the instability, the abuse I saw at a young age, us living in abandoned buildings, or with people I hardly knew, but what good would that do? I played the cards I was dealt; I lost some hands and won a few.

My mom let me down a few times. She wasn't who I wanted her to be, but I never doubted or questioned her love for me. I have only questioned some of her decisions, and now I realize I didn't even have that right. People make choices based on their options, and sometimes they don't have the best options. My mom never really had a lot of options. My mom was only nineteen years old when she was going through those things with Ray. I can't imagine being in that situation at nineteen. at that age, I felt like my life was just starting. It seemed like my mom had lived and experienced way more than an average teenager. I understood that then, and I understand that now. I honestly think that God blessed me with the sense of understanding at birth, at a very early age. I knew if my mom yelled at or disciplined me, it wasn't even about me, just the wrath of being a young, depressed mother. I understood if we didn't have money for things. I never asked for things, but I knew if I did, she would give them to me or at least try to. I understand who my mom was, and who I was, and how our lives were early on.

The flip side of that is this: parents should not expect children to understand. Children will sometimes pretend to understand or lie to their parents, because they do not want to upset their parents. Sometimes I wish I had the luxury of having the innocence of a child. Because I never had such innocence, I didn't take enough risks or chances. I couldn't allow myself to make too many mistakes, because I knew better. I don't know exactly when, but during childhood my heart died. I did not have natural feelings that other children had. I was serious all the time, and I always knew too much. All my friend's parents said I was too grown. I was too, because I had been affected by my environment. I was nonchalant and fearless. I was a straight shooter and could detect bullshit early on. I paid close attention to way people talked or expressed themselves, facial expressions, and their interactions with others. I was always cautious and non-trusting. I was that way because nothing was constant in my life. I had seen so much bad and not enough good, so the child in me never developed or manifested. She just slipped away.

Staring Through My Rearview

Fast forward. I was sitting in the car while my mom drove away from the hotel thinking a million different thoughts. I was so deep in thought that I didn't even realize we were at the river, right at the edge. The car was still moving, and my mom wasn't stopping. She looked completely out of it, so I yelled out "Mama!" she then smashed the brakes and yelled. Her tears just flowed. At that moment, my mom had lost it and decided that ending our lives was the only option. I don't know if it was a rash decision, or had she thought about it before. At the time, I couldn't process it. I jumped out the called Mr. Ruben; Mr. Ruben had deemed himself my godfather.

Mr. Ruben had been, and still was, a life saver for us. I knew Mr. Ruben's initial interest was my mom, but he soon found out he didn't have a chance and became a family friend. Mr. Ruben taught me about accounting, the bible, he knew a lot about education. He gave me a weekly allowance, took me to work or picked me up, and gave me money when I needed it. Many people thought he was a pervert, but he had never done anything that made me feel that way. I remember running up a phone bill, and he taught me all about contacting the company and paying my debt. The phone wasn't even in my name, but I kept that lesson with me. Mr. Ruben taught me a lot and came through for us many times. That's why I knew to call him. I told him what just happened. While I was talking, my mom was sitting in the car, crying.

Mr. Ruben showed up. and I know we were a sight to see! A car packed with clothes and food, a mom in the car, crying, her daughter outside the car spaced out, parked at the edge of the river. Mr. Ruben tried to get my mom out the car to talk, but she just yelled and told him to leave. My mom was mad that I had called him. I had let someone see her at her weakest moment.

We lived our lives like that, not really letting people know what was really going on in our world, pretending everything was fine, and trying not to accept handouts from anybody. I still have this trait today. I will not say it's good, but I will say it helped me become independent. Ironically enough, as a child I hated this trait that my mom had. I used to think, "Why do I have to suffer just so you can save face?" I thought it was selfish of her to turn down help, or not let anyone know that we needed help, because of pride. Being a mother now, I understand all too well. I remember how I felt and before I let my son feel this way, I would put my pride aside and ask for help. At seventeen years old, I didn't understand mental illness or depression. I did not know how to handle the situation afterwards, so we just never discussed it. We acted like it never happened.

I'm not sure how we left the river, but we ended up at my mom's friend house. Talbert was another life saver. My mom and Talbert had been on and off for several years. Talbert was a nice guy with a steady job. Talbert was older with adult children. I never really understood the relationship between

Talbert and my mom. My mom wasn't sure what she wanted. Talbert remained a good friend to her. Talbert gave her money, bought her things, and did things for me. I remember Talbert taking me to school one day. I refused to get out the car because my mom had put extensions in my hair. At a predominantly white school, I knew I would get made fun of. I was one of two blacks at the school. They did not know about hair extensions. Talbert gave me fifty dollars just so I could get out the car and he could get to work. I went into the school and loaded up on books at the book fair. My teacher questioned me about the amount of money and sent a note home to my mom about it. I got in a lot of trouble, but we laugh about it today. When we made it to Talbert's house, he tried to convince my mom to stay with him. I tried to convince her also. I was tired, and I had school and work the next day. I just wanted to go to bed. I still can't accurately describe that feeling that day. I couldn't figure out if my mom was going to kill us both, because she couldn't bear leaving me behind without her or she just may not have been in her right mind. I will never know, because we have never discussed that moment or day. In the black community having mental issues is taboo, or a joke, or just not discussed at all. If I had a handle on the situation, I would have reached out to get my mom some help. That day at the river was over, but the core of the problem stayed and manifested.

Running (Dying to Live)

As I sat in Talbert's basement ironing my work and school clothes, I realized what had really happened at the river. My mom was about to end it all, her life and mine. I realized a lot of things that night: I realized how severe my mom's mental state was, how you really can't depend on anyone, and that I wanted to get as far away from this life as possible. My mother was a young mother, so that, mixed with failed relationships, feeling unloved by her own parents and an everlasting stream of bad luck, made for an interesting life, to say the least. I made up my mind, my next day off from work, that I was going to talk to a recruiter about joining the Air Force. It was the end of my junior year; senior year was just around the corner. I had been accepted to several schools, but I knew that I couldn't afford those schools. My plan was to join the Air Force, because they could help pay for school and I could also make a living. The saying is, "If you want to make God laugh, tell him your plan." I learned this lesson too many times to count. I would like to think this was the first adult decision I ever made.

Senior year came, and I had everything set, I took the Armed Services Vocational Aptitude Battery Test (AVASB), passed, chose a job, and had a leave date: May 17th, 2004. My leave date was one day after my high school graduation; and I wanted it that way. The sooner I got out the better. I continued working at McDonald's but was growing tired of it. I had gotten a few raises but not enough for everything I was doing. I had gotten so good that I did the truck, grill, and cash register most nights by myself. Granted we were in a mall, so we didn't get a lot of customers, but I was still unhappy with the job. A guy that worked at the bookstore next door always stopped by, chatted with me, and always tried to get me to work for them. I usually said no, because I felt obligated to McDonald's and didn't want to leave them hanging. One day I decided to take him up on his offer and was hired the next day. I started working at the bookstore and enjoyed every minute of it. The problem was that I was only hired as a seasonal worker. The season ended, and I started working at Cracker Barrel with my friend, Erin. We enjoyed working together and planning what we were going to do when school let out. Prom came and went, and graduation was drawing near.

Finally, graduation came. My grandfather and aunt came from Chicago, and all my family nearby attended. I was so frazzled and trying to mentally prepare for leaving that everything kind of went by in a blur. A day after graduation, my mom, Arnetta, and my friend drove me to St. Louis for my flight to San Antonio. I remember thinking "this is it;" I'm going and never looking back. I was sworn in and got on a plane to Lackland Air Force Base. I remember when we first arrived, we had to call and let someone know that we were there and safe. My mom didn't have a phone, so I called my grandmother house, her number never changed, and I knew someone would be there. After I talked to my papa. I watched all the other girls who did not want to hang up, I thought they were crazy. I wasn't emotional at all.

    I realize now this may have been selfish. I was leaving my mom alone to handle life by herself, she had sacrificed so much for me, and all I could think about was leaving. But I honestly felt like being gone would be better for her; she could downsize and get an apartment, work any hours she wanted, and focus on herself. The reality is that leaving didn't help her at all, in a sense I think she lost her drive. I wasn't there to serve as motivation anymore; it's really easy to give up when you don't have someone looking at you for their next meal or a roof over their head. I left and things continued to go downhill for my mother. I think that only having to take care of you and only you should be the easiest thing in the world to do, but I learned and still learning that it's not that easy to some people

    The girls cried for their parents, children, or mates. I didn't cry for anyone. Sometimes these same girls cried all night long. Many had lied about having children, because they did not want to give legal custody of their children to anyone, so it was at night they snuck their pictures of their children out and cried. Many had married strangers so they wouldn't have to give up custody. In a sense, these women were making sacrifices, as they had also come from difficult situations. Many were older and had been out of high school for a while, couldn't find a job, and joining the military was the last option. Very few girls were fresh out of high school like me. I can honestly say that it was comical to go through what I had seen people in the military on TV endure. I never was bothered by the yelling; in fact, I did a lot of push-ups for busting out laughing all the time. I even became a squadron leader. As a squadron leader, if someone in your squad messed up, you had to do double the number of push-ups the person who messed up did. I just happened to have the oldest person in the squad in my group, a former flight attendant who couldn't do anything right. I did a lot of push-ups because of her. The drill sergeant would have her stand over and me and , "Look at what I made you do," I knew it was part of their mind games, so I never took it personally, but sometimes I wanted to strangle her as she slept. I did make a few friends. We talked about back home, and people we missed, and where we wanted to be stationed. I still remember some stories and faces vividly. I remember one girl being so tired of being yelled at that she asked me to drop a brick that was holding up a bed on her ankle, so she could be injured and sent home. I told her she was crazy and to pray instead. I wasn't about to intentionally harm anyone, and she would have only been sent to Med Hold anyway and back to training, we later found out. Med Hold is where they send you if you become injured or ill. You must wait in Med Hold until you can return to training or go home. I remember a tiny girl who reminded me of a cousin. She tried to commit suicide with a razor in the shower. She was sent to the psych floor. I am not sure if she did it to go home or was really dealing with some issues.

The military is very similar to the prison system; they follow some similar guidelines. You are told when to eat, sleep, use the bathroom, and speak. You scrub floors and polish shoes. You aren't allowed television or junk food, and you can't fraternize with the opposite sex. Someone is always watching and yelling at you if you make a mistake, and the money in the beginning almost amounts to the same amount that a person at McDonald's makes. I sometimes regretted my decision because I didn't like being controlled or being held responsible for someone else's mistake. Still I didn't want to go home. I knew nothing awaited me there but stress and despair, so I made a real effort to make it work without making too many mistakes. I eventually settled into a comfortable routine. In the month of June, San Antonio heat was almost smothering, and I had never felt anything like it in my life. I started to feel cramps in my stomach during Physical Training Exercise (PT). My sergeant sent me to the hospital to get checked out, because the stomach cramps had become unbearable. I underwent several tests to make sure the pain was just heat cramps and nothing else. I found out I had a hypoglycemia, a tilted pelvic, and cancer cells on my cervix. I had to call someone and let them know I was hospitalized. I wrote my grandpa, my mama, and my guy friend explaining everything. I eventually returned to training and things returned to normal. I received information about my location for technical school for my job and the additional testing I would need. The tests seemed normal, nothing to worry about.

One of the tests required me to receive shots of histamine. The reason for this test was to see how long I could breathe in the desert without having an allergy attack, or in my case, an asthma attack. I took the test; which was supposed to require six shots. I started to feel tightness in my chest, became short of breath, and started coughing uncontrollably after the third shot. I was having an asthma attack. I hadn't had an attack in years. As a child, I suffered from asthma terribly. It was so bad that everybody in the town knew I had asthma. I tried to play sports but couldn't for long because I would have an attack. When I begin high school, I stopped having attacks, stopped using my inhaler, and never went to a doctor's appointment for asthma. I was rushed to the hospital again. I thought I would return to training like before, I was told to report to Med Hold; Med Hold is where you go when you're sick and in training. In Med Hold some people are waiting to go home, and some are waiting to go back to their regular squadron. My situation was not determined. I continued restricted PT, went to meetings, doctor's appointments and wrote letters.

I didn't want to go home, but then I thought to myself, "I only came here to get away from my current situation". I had made an irrational decision in dire circumstances. I had run to the Air Force as an escape. I didn't really want to be part of the military institution. This was just a means to an end and a fast way out. I then realized that if I did get sent home, I would have a chance to do things over, not what I had to do. Finally, it was confirmed. I was going home. I was disappointed that I hadn't finished what I started, but now I planned to make this second chance count.

Guess Who's Back?

I returned home, and things weren't really all that different. My mom still didn't have a job. We moved into another house shortly after I returned. I partied with my cousins and friends, but I knew I had to think of a plan to leave this town. I had missed numerous college opportunities and deadlines because of my time in Basic Training, so my options were limited. I wondered to myself how things would have turned out if I went to school first.

One day I was speaking to my grandfather. He told me he knew some people at Chicago State University, and I should try applying there. I then figured out what I was going to do. I would move to Chicago, attend school, and help take care of him after he had surgery. I had been visiting Chicago since I was eight years old, and I loved my grandfather dearly. It seemed like the ideal situation, why not? People ask me if I was scared to move to Chicago at age 19. I wasn't. I didn't even think about the violence or cost of living. At the time, anywhere seemed better than home. I didn't have any fear. Having gone through all that I had gone through in my childhood, I was prepared for anything.

I caught the train to Chicago the very next week. I went to the university completed all my paperwork, got all the information, needed, and waited. Days went by and living with my grandpa didn't seem all that ideal anymore.

He had never really been a major part of my mother's life until I was born, so he wasn't used to sharing his life or space with anyone. I wasn't really used to him either. I couldn't stand his cigarette smoke, he didn't clean that well, and he yelled a lot. My grandfather and I have an unbreakable bond now, but we could never live together. I can talk to him about anything. My grandfather had always showed me respect and engaged in my ideas, even as a child. I love him. I used to think to myself, "Here we were with this great relationship and he had missed out on my mom's life totally." My mom resented my relationship with my grandfather, but I understood. I understood that I was a constant reminder of everything she failed to achieve. I have heard it said that you have to sometimes give up your life so your children can have a life; I truly think that is what my mom did. I realize now that she did the best, she could with what she had.

Unfortunately, this closeness put a strain on everyone. Everything he was to me, my mom needed him to be to her. My grandfather was used to being a bachelor and I was trying to be independent. I had to re-think this situation. I decided I would go back home and work until school began. I had fees and expenses that I knew I couldn't depend on anyone else to pay but me. I went home again.

When I returned to my mom's house, my cousin, Arnetta, came over to stay with me at my mom's house. We grew up together, got our first job together, and if you saw her you saw me. We started job hunting everywhere. Eventually, she began at a nursing home. I began working at a restaurant, and we both returned to our old job at McDonald's. We had two jobs and a plan! I would work, save money, and pay my college fees and then leave for school. She would work, save money, and then move to Atlanta. I had to quit the job at the restaurant because I couldn't deal with the racism. She quit the job at the nursing home because she couldn't deal with the smell. We at McDonald's during the week and partied on the weekend. We also kicked my mother some cash, because she wasn't having us staying there for free. My mother was working minimum-wage jobs that were not stable.

In December, I sent my entire check $247 to Chicago University to pay for my dorm-room fees. I then had to figure out how I was going to pay for other expense and get to Chicago. I didn't want anyone's help. I did buy a few things on my list, and my grandmother gave me a comforter-set to take, and my aunt gave me a calling card. I went to the Salvation Army and bought a red- and -black plaid set of suitcases. I was a first-generation college student. My mom never finished school. She dropped out in the ninth grade I wasn't sure about my father, because I had never met him. I didn't have anybody to tell me what to expect. I had to figure everything out on my own. This wasn't a problem, as I was used to figuring things out on my own. I did however learn from a stranger in the University's library how to fill out financial aid paperwork.

I quit my job and then reserved my train ticket for January 2nd. Two days before I was supposed to leave something happened that made me realize I needed to leave quickly. My cousin and her boyfriend had gotten into an argument, somehow, he involved me, and I attacked him with a knife. The people that were around, grabbed me, telling me no. I had cut him on the face. His injuries were not major. The police were called; I ran to a friend's house, slept it off, and went home the next day so I could leave for Chicago. I realized that things could have turned out differently that night. I could have been arrested, gotten a record, or I could have killed him. I could have ruined my chance of going to college by being in the wrong place at the wrong time. January 2nd came, and it was time. I knew I wasn't coming back. I told everybody "I could be broke on the streets of New York and I'm never coming back to this place"

When the train pulled into Chicago, I could see the sign that read Chicago State University on its lawn. It was like a sign of refuge. I thought, "That's where my life is going to begin, the place where I am going to make things happen at." I look back now and laugh at myself; I had no idea about the journey ahead. I went to Chicago State University to become a lawyer. I had the characteristics of a lawyer is what people told me. I read books all the time and was opinionated. As a child, I watched the movie A Time to Kill and was hooked. Matthew McConaughey plays a lawyer who gets a father off who avenged the brutal rape of his daughter. The rapists had gotten off free. I wanted to fight for social injustice. I wanted to put the bad guys away. I had no idea the actual fight that lay ahead.

Shit Don't Stop

Here I was in the city of big shoulders, the windy city. It was January, so the wind was whipping across my face, I stood there taking it all in, not knowing what to expect. I had spent so much money just getting there; I knew the first order of business had to be getting a job. The only money I had in my pocket was the money given to me by a good friend named Shanelle. Shanelle was a friend I had met through my friend Erin. We had hung out senior year and during the summer. Shanelle also left town and went to school somewhere else. As I got off the train, I realized that I was completely on my own now. Thank God for the money Shanelle gave me because it came in handy. I bought a backpack, iron, and other toiletries. I went to stay with my grandfather for a week until it was time for me to move in the dorms.

The day came for me to move in the dorms and my uncle Freddy and my uncle Bobby came to pick me up to take me to the university. We arrived at the dorms; I remember thinking to myself, this ugly brown building is a dorm? I saw all the other students getting moved in and set up with their parents; their parents had driven them there and moved them in. I didn't have the same luxury, I came on the train, my uncles were moving me in, and my mom didn't drive me up there because she didn't have a car at the time. I felt like an orphan or a ward of the state. I brushed the feeling off and got settled into my room. I didn't have time to feel sorry for myself.

My first of three roommates was a character to say the least. I had to go through two roommates before I finally got along with one. My first roommate had a friend that seemed a little weird, but I never really paid them no mind. The friend started getting on my nerves, she would stay in our room all night staring and talking about her roommate. I told our Dorm room manger or("tricked" on them, as they called it in Chicago.) I had early classes, and unlike them I actually went to class, so I needed my rest. Eventually, I met Amanda and she was nothing like they made her out to be. She and I clicked immediately. We were from the same area and had the same sense of humor. I could tell that she wasn't really like they were portraying her to be. I noticed that, even though they talked about Amanda negatively, they still pretended to like her. Well, I told Amanda how they really felt about her. Amanda was hurt by the fact that they were two-faced, but she got it over it, and we came up with a plan. We were going to leave our current roommates and room with each other. We moved to the third floor and everything was cool. Amanda was homesick a lot and hardly went to class, but she was and still is the sweetest person I know.

In the dorms we had what they called Suites, two rooms that shared a bathroom. While I was still with my first roommate, I became friends with my suitemate, Lois. I saw Lois in the common area heating up food. I noticed she had a military uniform on, so we talked about the military, and the conversation went from there. Lois asked if I wanted to go to IHOP and I said yes, this was kind of unusual for me because I wasn't used to meeting people and jumping in the car with them. Lois and I had many things in common, and we started hanging out. She was from Chicago, studying to become a nurse.

Amanda and I had a good time as roommates, and our circle of friends grew. Eventually my friends became hers and vice versa. We formed a crew" Me, Amanda, Lois, Bernita, Tammy, Shonta, and me.

The crew went everywhere together. I learned a lot from these women. We all came up with ways to pay for snacks, laundry, and transportation. Most of the time we sold our books back, and other times we just used whatever boy that liked us. I remember the semester began, my financial aid paperwork wasn't completed, leaving me without a book voucher. We looked around campus for signs about people selling books. One guy wanted me to meet him somewhere to get a book. The girls were like "uh uh we are coming with you." We met the guy who did seem creepy, but I got the book. I also learned how to take public transportation from Bernita and Shonta. I refused to keep calling my grandpa to take me places and I didn't have a car. I had to learn how to get around on my own.

I was the mean one in the crew to hear everybody else tell it. I admit I had a no-nonsense attitude. Most of my peers were just getting their first taste of freedom and independence. I had been in the military, been going to clubs since I was 17, and had gained my independence early. I thought many people in the dorms were immature. We used to go to other people's "room" parties, but nobody was allowed in our room. I just wasn't having it. One day I ran into one of my old friends from back home named Nick. I used to hang out with Nick when I was a teenager back in Missouri. Nick and I linked up that day, and it was just like old times, I knew we would stay in touch. He also had family in Chicago and had moved there. Nick looked out for me and checked on me on the regular. I felt a little more comfortable knowing he was around. Nick turned out to be a big help during my stay in Chicago. Some was good help, and some was bad help. Nick was a street guy, and he was smart, I knew his parents, and he knew mine. We knew the same people back home, so we were like family.

Spring Break came, so I went home. I received a call while at home about my financial aid. I had a "business hold" on my account because of my financial aid paperwork. I had no idea what the problem could be, but I knew I had to find out. When I returned to school, I found out that the problem was my mom's tax information. She had been married since I was twelve years old, but she and my stepfather had been separated for years. My stepfather was retired and made good money, so that was figured in with my financial aid. The school wanted to me to prove that my stepfather's income was not my mother's income. I made several calls trying to rectify this situation. If I didn't get this cleared up, my financial aid would be denied, and I would have to quit school.

I tried calling my mom to explain the problem. I called my grandmother and cousins every day, trying to get them to contact her. My mom sent papers, but that wasn't enough. The school did not want to give me any aid, because papers from my mom and stepfather made it seem like they had a lot of money, so my EFC was extremely high. EFC means Expected Family Contribution. In my case, I didn't have a "family" that could contribute to the cost of my education. I needed my mom to prove she was separated from her husband and to also account for all the income she claimed on her tax returns. I didn't have any luck getting her to cooperate. I thought that maybe she was still mad because I had left. Maybe she didn't realize the importance of education.

I soon found out she was too pre-occupied with her drug- using boyfriend. My mom had met a guy on a chat -line and moved him in right before I left for school. He was on drugs, and he and my mother were being evicted and moving around a lot. Therefore, I could never get in touch with her. This caused me to recall what had happened when mid-terms were coming up. I had caught pneumonia, probably from stressing over school and running around in the cold weather looking for jobs. I called my mother because I couldn't afford the medicine; my mother said she would ask my stepfather for the money. I never heard back from her, but later my stepfather called and asked if I had gotten the medicine because he gave my mother money for the medicine. I told him no and then called my mother. I asked, "why didn't she give me the money?" Her reply was, "I do what I want to do with my money." I knew then she was being influenced by something or someone. I felt so angry! How could she treat her only child this way? Why would she use her sickness to get money from someone and then use it for herself? Mr. Reuben sent me the money, and I walked to Walgreens to get the medicine. As if things couldn't any worse, I found out the university was charging me out-of-state tuition. I was being charged double what my peers were being charged; the fact that I had stayed with my grandfather and used his address didn't matter. The university used the state that my mom had filed taxes in, Missouri. I didn't have a lot of options at this point. It seemed like all of us started having financial problems or personal problems at the same time. Everybody had to start thinking about ways to solve our issues.

This Ain't Living

At this point I realized that I was grown. I could no longer depend on mama or daddy or anybody. I had to take care of business on my own. I felt alone but not discouraged. I then hearing about a program called CRCP, it was a program that allowed students to work for United Postal Service and they would help with school, books, and transportation. CRCP seemed like the very thing that I needed. Amanda, my friend had tried it and quit the first day. Bernita and I figured we would try it. We had to travel 90 minutes away for the interview process. We made it to the interview, got everything completed, but didn't realize we had missed our ride out there. We were an hour and a half away from the city, with no money, no phones and no idea how to get back. I had memorized Amanda's number and we called her. I knew if anybody could help us figure something out, she could. Amanda was resourceful like that. We waited until day turned to dark, and finally! There was Amanda in the car with Shontae. Shantae's car was beat up, and they weren't sure if they could make it, but they did, and we were saved.

Bernita and I were accepted into the program. I would work from pm to am and Bernita worked am to pm. We had transportation to and from work. They even gave us a pass, so we could ride on the bus and train for free. I remember the first day I was like "Oh I can load these small brown trucks," what I didn't know was that we also had to load the long white trailers. I felt like I was working in a sweat shop! Bells were going off. Supervisors were constantly yelling, and soot was everywhere. I kept getting bruises from the belt. I would work until 4, get home at 5:30, get a few hours of sleep, and go to my summer class at eight am. This worked out for a while, and I was at ease, I was getting a little money every week and I didn't have to worry about getting kicked out of school.

One night at work I was loading, and I realized it was time for me to go. I told my supervisor I had to leave. He asked me if I could build a few more walls. I said no because I had to leave. I had to catch the bus that took me directly back to the dorms. If I missed the bus, I wouldn't have a way home.

The supervisor and I started arguing, During the argument, he stated "I can't help it your parents didn't plan a better life for you." I was fuming mad at this point, but I calmed down and walked away. I got my things out my locker and ran outside, and the bus had left me! I was devastated. It was four in the morning and I was stuck somewhere with no idea how to get home. I saw a few people that were regular workers outside, who were not a part of the program. They told me a Pace bus would come in about thirty minutes, so I waited.

The Pace finally came, and they took me as far as allowed. I ended up at the Red Line on 95th and State, that was as close as I could get to the dorms, so I had to walk the remaining four blocks. When I crossed the street going to the other side of the station a young man appeared at my side. He looked no more than 20, maybe 21. He had a wild look in his eyes. I thought he was going to try and grab me and rape me. He showed me a gun and told me to give him my bag. I handed it over right away, and he took off running. I was too tired to care. The only things in the bag were my work ID, two dollars, and my asthma pump. I had been robbed at gunpoint and wasn't even bothered by it. I was just happy he didn't kill me. I then walked to the dorms cursing myself the entire way. The sun was coming up, and the construction the school was doing made it hard to get to the dorms. When I finally made it to the dorms and fell out, I didn't go to class at 8am and I didn't return to CRCP. I told my friends what happened, but I left out the robbery part, because I didn't want them to be spooked out. I didn't tell my family until years later. I knew if my grandma and mom found out, they would have come to Chicago and made me come home. They assumed everything they saw on the news about Chicago happened where I stayed. I appreciated their concern, but I couldn't stress enough that I was now an adult in an adult world. I informed the person in charge of the program that I would not return unless I could get a different shift. This did not happen, so I quit. I still regret that decision. One part of me felt like there was no way I should put myself in that position again but the other part of me felt like I should have toughed it out.

How was I going to pay for school now? My mother still wasn't doing her part, so I had to take care of myself. Bernita had similar issues with her mother, so she told me some tricks of the trade, and I was able to take care of a few situations myself. I had financial aid send my mother's information to my email instead of my mothers' and I completed her part myself. I finally got everything worked out, but it still wasn't enough for me to stay in school or in the dorms. I couldn't get out of paying out-of state tuition, and CRCP refused to pay all their money because I had left the program. It was now summer, so Amanda had gone home. It was just Bernita, Lois, and me taking summer classes. I couldn't afford to stay in the dorms or school anymore. Lois didn't want to keep taking out loans to stay in the dorms anymore, and Bernita to leave.

Ambitions AZ A Ridah

Lois, Bernita, and I began hunting for apartments; we looked online and walked around neighborhoods we knew nothing about. Bernita preferred the West Side where she was from, but Lois and I preferred the South side because that's where the school was located. We decided that Bernita would get her own place, and Lois and I would get our own place together. We found a place for $650, two bedrooms, security, right by the L. I thought this was the perfect spot. We contacted the leasing office, saw the apartment, and figured out how much money we had to pay. Then one day the person we were working with on the apartment just disappeared. We contacted the leasing office and they told us we should be glad he stopped contacting us, because he was a thief and had been stealing money from prospective tenants. (We found out later the only reason he didn't get us was because he knew Lois's brother.)

We had to come up with $650 each for the apartment. I had a few UPS checks saved, and Lois had some reserve money coming in. We still didn't have enough, so we sat around thinking of how to get the money. (I'm not impressed by people who do things under comfortable circumstances or look for someone to help them all the time) I realized early on that you have to get out here and make moves for yourself and in the words of my late great-grandmother, "If you don't got, don't nobody got either "I thought about how

I had a lots of jewelry from school that I never really wore. I suggested to Lois that maybe we could Pawn some stuff to get the money. Lois agreed. We drove around Chicago all day, hot and sweaty, looking for pawn shops. We even asked my grandpa where a few were, but he did not offer any help. I was not even upset about it, nor did I expect anything from anyone. We finally found a pawn shop, and pawned a few things, but didn't get what we were expecting. I was sad that I had to pawn some of the jewelry; some of it had sentimental meaning to me. I didn't feel sorry for myself too long though, the clock was ticking, and we had to be out the dorms soon, and we needed to secure the apartment.

    We had almost had enough. I finally broke down and asked my grandmother and another friend of mine in the military for help. They both sent money, and I promised to pay them back. In August of 2005, we moved into our apartment with what little we had in the dorms. I only had my clothes when I moved from the dorms. My papa was coming to Chicago, and he said he would drop off some things from my mom's house to me because I didn't even have a TV. (My papa is my grandmother's husband; my grandpa is my mother's father.) I moved in with a small TV, comforter set, clothes, and an air mattress, and Lois pretty much had the same. The first few days in our apartment were extremely hot, we didn't have central air, or an air conditioner, and we were on the third floor. Third floors in Chicago during the summer are the worst. Heat rises, and the walls and floor sweat. Days passed, and I couldn't take it anymore. I called my grandmother crying, asking her for money for an air conditioner. She sent the money, and my grandpa took me to buy it. Lois was able to get a few more air conditioners from her parents' house that they no longer lived in, and everything was fine after that. Lois's fiancé tried putting one of the air conditioners in the living room and dropped it from our third-floor window. We all just stood there with our mouths open; we couldn't believe it.

The more we told people where we moved, the stranger looks we received. We had moved to one of Chicago's worst neighborhoods, Englewood. It was so bad that Lois's fiancé's father came to bless our home with bless oil for our protection. I'm glad that we had Lois fiancé family in our lives. They were nice people and invited us to their church. During these hard times we were having, church and God were the only ways to turn to sometimes. I remember Lois's fiancés mother taking me places to apply for jobs. The only thing she wanted in return was for me to attend church with her, so I did. We attended church regularly. Too this day, I watch it every Sunday and pay my tithes online.

I wasn't in school anymore, unlike Lois. I still hung out on campus with everybody, trying to figure out how to get back in. I heard that the

University's bookstore was hiring, so I applied. I got the job. Everything was going well. The pay was decent, and because I was willing to come in very early, I got all the hours I wanted. A lot of us were hired to meet the needs when the fall semester rush began. It was busy all day. We really didn't handle much money because most students were paying with book vouchers. I had the job, but I still hadn't worked out my financial situation. The money I was making wasn't enough to afford for school. It was barely enough to pay the bills that Lois and I split. The manager at the bookstore questioned me about my class schedule, and I gave him a fake schedule. If he found out I wasn't a student, I would lose my job. When the rush came to an end, the manager started letting people go. My manager said that I was a great worker and that he wanted to keep me on. I was relieved. I should have known that string of good luck wouldn't last. Somehow my manager found out about the situation with CRCP and that I wasn't in school anymore. I was fired.

Got My Mind Made Up

Here I was again, no job: worrying about school, paying rent and other bills. I resumed my job search, and it wasn't easy because, the more I looked, the colder the weather became. I had always heard about Chicago's winters but had never experienced one. My first winter in Chicago was horrible! I got lost a lot in the middle of nowhere trying to get to an interview and I caught pneumonia a second time. I applied for jobs everywhere. I was still getting help from Mr. Ruben and my grandparents, but not enough to pay bills. My grandfather started feeling sorry for me. He wanted me to focus on getting back in school, so he made an agreement with my grandmother. They would each pay half of my rent while I looked for a job. My half of the rent was $325, so they paid $162 each. I tried getting private loans but needed co-signers. Arnetta and my grandmother tried to be co-signers for me but were unable. Everything I tried kept falling apart. I couldn't catch a break.

One day, I was hanging out on campus with Amanda, and we thought of an idea. We had heard about a few girls that were students and exotic dancers. Everybody had seen the movie *Players Club* and was convinced that they could pull it off just like in the movie. So, I then started thinking I could go that route too, just until I found a job. Amanda and I went to the beauty supply store, bought wigs, and other things like make-up and jewelry. Amanda said she would work there as a host, and I was going to work there to be a dancer. I had never done anything like this in my life, and I really didn't think I had the nerves to do it, but I was willing to try anything at this point. I waited for a day that Amanda would be free. She and I took the train downtown to a place that we had found on the internet. I didn't want to go to a place near the school or where I could run into anybody I knew. (Ironically, years later, I would work for a company two buildings from this very same place.) Amanda and I arrived, it was quiet, dark, and smelled musky. The lady asked Amanda and me for our ID's, she then slid them through some machine and replied, "Nice fakes." Amanda and I looked at each shocked; we knew the ID's were real. I took that as a sign, and suggested we get out of there, the moment we walked in I knew we didn't belong there. It seemed like every time I was about to do something I shouldn't, God always blocked it. We laughed about it, got on the train, and headed home.

I wish I could say that was the only thing shameful I did during that time, but it wasn't, Desperate times calls for desperate measures, and I was going through a rough time. One night we were all hanging out in Amanda's room. There was guy that liked me hanging out with us. Somehow, we started talking about how Amanda and I went to the strip club. The guy that liked me said that he would pay me to dance for him any day. I blurted out, "you can pay me now" I was only joking, but he said that he would, and. I was thinking "oh shit, he is serious. "I asked him how much he would pay. He said fifty dollars. I was like "well that's not bad for a lap dance," the girls at the club only getting ten. He said we could do it in Amanda's room, so that's where we went. I didn't take off my clothes, and the dance lasted three minutes, and he did pay me fifty dollars. I couldn't believe I did it. Amanda and our other friends were waiting outside the door. I think they thought something else was going down, but nothing else happened. The money came in handy, so I didn't feel all that bad about it. The guy and I stayed friends. He helped me out with my electricity bill a few weeks after that, but I never kissed him or had sex with him. This same guy used to sleep in the room with me when Amanda and I were roommates. He didn't live in the dorms, but he was always up there hanging out. He was sweet on me, but I didn't trust him because he was sneaky. We slept in the same bed plenty of times but never had sex.

True enough, we lived in Englewood, but it turned out to be the best situation for me. We lived not even a block from the train station, so I could get anywhere without going far. I remember my aunt suggesting that I move closer to home, In Illinois. My reply was, "I didn't go through all this just to run back home. I got to make it count for something. If I was going to run, it would have been early on." I had learned too much, experienced too much, and sacrificed too much to just run back home. As I said before, location was key, and our apartment was right next door to Kennedy-King College. One day I was getting off the train from another long journey for an interview. I decided to visit Kennedy-King. I heard things about it. They weren't good, but it was worth looking into. I went inside, looked around, and asked for more information. I spoke to someone in student services who explained the enrollment process to me. During the explanation, I found out that I couldn't transfer there because I needed transcripts from Chicago State University.

I couldn't get transcripts from the them because I owed them $5000. I went home and thought about the situation. I knew I couldn't pay the University. I came up with a solution. I wouldn't tell Kennedy-King about Chicago State. I would start completely over. I really did not want to do that. I had worked hard at Chicago State and earned good grades, and I didn't want to take the same classes again. At this point I didn't have a choice, it was either start over or stay out of school while time passed me by. I came to Chicago to attend school, and that's what I was going to do. It might have not been my ideal school or situation, but it was school.

Kennedy-King had a reputation for being ghetto and hood. I never cared about the rumors, because I knew what I had to do. I enrolled at Kennedy-King as if I have never been to school. I was back at square one, starting all over again. I learned that because Kennedy-King's tuition was so much cheaper, I would get money back from financial aid every semester. I didn't have to take out any loans, because grants paid for everything. The new situation was beneficial to me, but I still felt sad and disappointed. I didn't come all the way to Chicago to attend a junior college. I hated not finishing what I started, and I hated owing people. I decided that the money I received from financial aid would go to pay Chicago State what I owed.

Kennedy-King is a two-year college so if I was going to become a lawyer like I planned to, I would eventually have to enroll in a university and obtain a bachelor's degree. So, I had to clear my debt. I remember telling Lois, she said "So you are just going to start over" I was like "yep and this time I'm going to make straight A's." My first semester, I made straight A's. I can honestly say that some of my best professors were at Kennedy-King.

I had an English professor that truly brought out the writer in me. I loved writing papers in my English 101 class and receiving feedback from the professor. He gave me some of the best constructive criticism and helped me do more descriptive writing. I had taken Advanced Language Skills and Academic Composition in high school, so I wrote well. but it wasn't until college that I really took my time writing. I did well in my English class; in fact, my professor published one of my essays in his journal, *Expressions From Englewood*. My essay was about Tupac Shakur. *Expressions From*

Englewood Is a collection of journals that feature essays, poems, and fiction stories from people that live and work in the Englewood community. My essay was in the first volume. There has been seven volumes published since. I am Facebook friends with my former English professor. He is still the editor and the journal is doing well. I was excited when I first saw the book. I couldn't believe something I had written had been published. I asked for extra copies to give to my family members, I was proud of it. I'm glad that I was a part of something special.

I also had the same Criminal Justice professor for every criminal justice class, and that was my decision. Professor Byers was a clean-cut, tall, African American man. He was always dressed sharply from head to toe and oozed charisma. I think most women took his class just to look at him. I thought he was attractive too, but I took his classes because he was smart. He actually understood the system and how it was to be black in America. Byers wasn't a professor that taught from a textbook. He taught from experience. Byers made the lesson relatable to what was going on around us. Byers was an attorney. I was like a sponge in his class, soaking up everything I could from him. I felt like he really cared that we understood the system and what we were up against. I was in his class when "Jenna Six "happened. Byers and some of his colleagues raised money and put together a trip together where we would attend the march for the Jenna Six. Unfortunately, I couldn't go because I had to work.

I can't write about my professors at Kennedy-King and leave out the one professor that gave me the only B that I had ever received during my college career. Professor Davis was known for being a hard-ass. All the students avoided taking his sociology class. I couldn't get past taking his class; he was the only one teaching at night. I tried to ignore all the rumors I heard about him and go in with an open mind. I figured if I practiced the same discipline, I had in all my other classes, I would be fine. I was also taking English 102 at the time, and my professor in that class said to me, "My frat brother is going to fail you." I asked who he was referring to, and he said Professor Davis. I asked him why, and he said, "He fails everybody, especially the ones like you." I told him there was no way I was going to fail.

The first day in class, I noticed right away that he had a dry personality, and it seemed like every little thing irritated him. I really wasn't concerned about his attitude. I just wanted to be treated fairly. I worked hard in his class, but nothing seemed good enough for him. I would raise my hand to answer questions, and he would wait until someone else volunteered. I couldn't understand him. The other students didn't even try, and when the middle of semester came, we only had five students left in class. Professor Davis talked about today's youth having it so easy. I think that's what bothered him about the students. He felt like we had it too easy, so he made it hard on us. I continued to do my best in his class. I still received a "B" as my final grade. The other students and professors thought that grade was a big deal, but I was upset, I was trying to maintain my 4.0. grade point average.

Time went by and I began making friends at Kennedy-King. I can honestly say these friends were different from my friends at the university. The students at Kennedy-King were from my neighborhood or the surrounding areas. So, they had a lot more "street sense." One day I told a classmate that I was looking for a job. She told me to apply at her job doing homecare. At first, I couldn't see me doing anything in the health care field. It just wasn't my area. But she told me I would get hired. The work was not hard she said, but the pay was minimum. I thought about it decided to try it; anything was better than nothing, and I didn't want my grandparents to keep paying my rent. I went downtown and applied for the job. I was hired immediately and told what day to report for orientation. I was excited; I felt like I was finally getting back on track. I was in school and working. I made up my mind to bite the bullet and start over, and it was starting to work out.

Changes

This new job required me to go to elderly people's homes and help to cook and clean up. I was assigned a lady named Mrs. Howard that lived close to my apartment. Mrs. Howard was a character. It seemed like every time I went to her home something was happening. When I first visited her house, I found the police there. A man had tried to break into Mrs. Howard's home through the laundry-room window. Her apartment was in the basement of her son's apartment building, So, when the robber stuck his head through the window, Mrs. Howard wheeled into the laundry room and caught- him. She hit him with a hatchet! She had hatchets everywhere in her house. I found them stuffed in the furniture, cabinets, and in her bathroom. I thought to myself," This lady is crazy! Mrs. Howard turned out to be nice, I would arrive there at 8a.m. and leave at 12. I really didn't do much but fix breakfast for her and help her take a bath. We talked about everything; she loved the fact that I was from down south and loved comparing stories.

When my first pay day arrived, I had to go downtown to get my check. I was on the train going home, and I noticed a guy motioning with his hands trying to get my attention. I ignored him. The train was packed. I was tired, and I wasn't about to entertain this guy. When I got home, I realized my check was gone. I also realized my bag was open. The guy was trying to tell me I was being pick-pocketed. Someone had stolen my check from my bag. I was sick. It was my first check, and the entire thing was supposed to pay my rent. I didn't know what to do; I called Lois and told her what happened. We called the leasing office and they told us that we would have to pay a late fee. I called my supervisor and I was told to file a police report and they would issue me another check. I did and my job reissued a replacement check. (I never take purses on the train anymore. To this day especially when I travel to Chicago; my purse is always in my suitcase.)

I was glad Lois didn't get upset when she found out I didn't have my part of the rent. Lois and I had similar qualities, which is why we got along so well. We were not afraid of hard work. Whenever we got an idea, we ran with it. We didn't want anybody thinking we needed help, so we always tried to handle things on our own. I valued Lois when she agreed to go to the pawn shop. I knew if she had the go-getter instinct she had while we were hustling for money to get our apartment, she would be responsible when we got it. We weren't totally alike in all areas though. We had different family backgrounds. Lois came from a two-parent household and had a big family. I was an only child raised by a single mother. Lois and I really didn't have any major conflicts as roommates. At the same time, I think it worked out so well with Lois and I because we were never home. We were always away at work or school; sometimes we didn't even know when the other was home. We only depended on each other to pay the bills. Lois had a car, but I never asked her for rides to places I needed to go. I took the train or the bus everywhere. I would ride with her if we were going in the same direction, but for the most part I took public transportation most of the time.

Lois introduced me to a guy named Tim. He was a student at Chicago State University, and we knew the same people. At first, I thought Tim was an asshole. I used to come home see him there and pay him no mind. (That's funny to me now because Tim is one of my best guy friends today.) I remember coming home from school one day tired, and Tim and another friend were sitting in the living room. I was uncomfortable, because I wanted to come home, take a shower, and just go to bed. I didn't want to shower while they were there. I asked Lois to come into my room and talk. I explained how I felt, and she understood.

I would like to say we handled all our conflicts easily, but we didn't. I, like my mom, always wanted my living space cleaned. Lois, however, wasn't much of a cleaner. Her room was junky, and she really didn't feel the need to clean until something was extremely dirty. I was not used to that. I used to clean the apartment by myself, but then Lois and her fiancé would act like we were still in the dorms. I became irritated with this one day and started putting signs all over the place. The signs told them what to clean and when to clean it. Lois and her fiancé didn't like that. She took the signs down. Eventually Lois got better about the cleaning. One other conflict we had was about food. I bought the foods I liked and cooked them, and Lois and her fiancé bought what they liked and cooked. Sometimes I would come home and find that my food had been eaten by Lois's fiancé. I never knew when they were home, so I wrote them a note. I told them how I felt about my food being eaten, and how they did not clean up. I was taking the train to grocery shop, the last thing I needed was someone eating my food. Lois wrote a note back defending their ways. I didn't care much about the response letter. Eventually Lois and her fiancé replaced the food

Tim came around a lot, and we would all hang out together. One day, Tim asked if I wanted to buy a gun. Without hesitation I said yes. I went to the school's ATM, got the money, and bought the gun from him. I felt like two women living in Englewood needed a gun protection. Lois wasn't all that thrilled about a gun being in our apartment, but she didn't make a big deal out of it. I made sure I took all the legal steps I needed to take to own a gun, so I was cool with it.

Trading War Stories

Englewood had been abandoned because of the foreclosure crisis and shrinking tax tolls. The investors and residents left the neighborhood after the crisis, leaving nothing but abandoned buildings and vacant lots. Drug dealers used the abandoned buildings to hide drugs. Addicts used these buildings to do drugs, and sexual predators used them to rape people. The residents remaining in Englewood felt forgotten. But they regained some hope when a few more apartment buildings were built and a new campus for Kennedy-King College were built. Englewood is stuck in what sociologists may call a poverty trap. Englewood is one of the most dangerous neighborhoods in the city by almost every metric: violent crime, property crime, and quality-of-life crime. In 2014, Englewood was ranked eighth out of 77 community areas in Chicago for violent crime, fifth among Chicago areas in property crime, and 8th out of 100 for quality of life crimes. Police commanders and gang initiatives have come and gone through the years, but Englewood just continues to get more violent and the criminals more brazen. Residents have reported that they sleep bathtubs to protect themselves from bullets. This is where Lois and I had chosen to live.

Lois and I had been in our apartment about six months, we became friends with our maintenance guy, an Arab named Ashraf. Ashraf was a jack of all trades. He fixed things, worked on computers, sold furniture, worked at the liquor and the dollar store, and leased apartments. Ashraf helped us with everything. We had been sleeping on air mattresses for the past six months, and when Ashraf mentioned that he sold furniture, we instantly became interested. Ashraf told us we could get a frame, mattress, and box spring for $100. The tricky part was driving all the way out West to get them, and getting them back, because we couldn't afford delivery. Lois had a small, green, Toyota Tercel, and she was convinced that we could move them on her car. I went along with it. I was tired of my air mattress, and we headed out West for the beds. Ashraf friends helped us tie the mattresses down onto the roof, and the frames were put in the backseat, hanging out the windows. I was sure we were going to get pulled over by the cops. When we made it all the way back to the South Side, we realized we had another dilemma. How were we going to get the beds upstairs? We stayed on the third floor. We stood outside pondering, until we just said, "forget it"., we would move them one by one ourselves. We moved the beds as the neighborhood guys watched. (A few guys offered to help, but we didn't accept. My biggest fear was someone breaking into our apartment.) It felt so good sleeping on a real bed after being on air mattresses for so long.

I was back in the swing of things. I was back in school and working. I worked for Mrs. Howard in the morning and went to school in the evenings. The neighborhood guys would mess with me, calling me "Schoolgirl." In fact, I had a lot of nicknames in the neighborhood: Red, Pretty Girl, Wife, and Baby Mama. I don't think anyone ever knew my real name. Lois's nickname was roommate; she got that nickname because I was always telling the guys to get off my roommate's car. We might have been living in one of Chicago's worst neighborhoods, but we never felt its wrath. Living in Englewood was a huge benefit to us. The rent was cheap. It was in central location. It wasn't small, and my school was across the street from my apartment. I will not say it was all peaches and creams, because there were tragedies.

I hated coming home after a long day of work and school and having to walk around dice games. I hated the fact that nobody delivered food over there, and the fact that we only received mail on Friday, if at all. We heard about things happening in our neighborhood all the time on the news or from other people, but we never considered moving. I remember walking home one night from class, getting to my corner, and a guy told me to stop walking and just wait a second. The guy was a dude that we had seen on the regular around the neighborhood, so I trusted him somewhat. Lois and I had nicknamed him "Dresser" A character from *The Five Heartbeats,* because he also had a raspy voice. I looked at him like he was crazy, but something told me to listen. I waited at the corner, and about a minute later I heard gun shots. The guys were having a shoot-out. I couldn't believe it. I didn't know when it was safe to walk down the block to my apartment, because Dresser had taken off running. I stood at the corner making sure everything was clear. Eventually Lois and her fiancé appeared on the sidewalk and I walked towards them to our building. The police arrived to question us, seeing if we had saw anything, I had seen it all, but I couldn't name anyone that was shooting., Honestly even if I could have I wouldn't. Living in the hood taught me to mind my own business.

I wasn't really shaken up about the shooting; I had seen someone get killed in my grandpa's neighborhood before. I was looking out the window one night, watching a group of guys walk by. They entered an alley and suddenly, they started shooting at one guy. The guy fell dead, and they ran off. My loud screams woke my grandfather. He jumped up, gun in his hand, looking bewildered. I told him what I had seen, he told me to stay away from the window and to never scream like that again. I wasn't shaken about the shooting that day, until the police removed a bullet from a tree in front of our building. I couldn't count how many times I had walked by that tree, if it hadn't been for that Dresser, I could have been shot dead that day. We eventually became familiar with the residents and they became familiar with us. They knew we went back and forth to work and school all day. They knew we were young, lived alone. I constantly worried that something would happen to one of us.

A lot of the guys looked out for us or tried to be nice. I didn't deal with them at all, but Lois did. I would come outside and find her checking blood pressures or offering the guys food. She was extremely too nice to them. I knew we were dealing with killers and drug dealers and I didn't want anything to do with them. I did eventually see Dresser again. I continued to see Dresser on the block and he always called me "Pretty "Girl. Then one day I noticed I hadn't seen him in a while. I was walking home from school one day, and I noticed a few people wearing t-shirts with pictures on them. I asked another guy from the block who it was, and as I got closer, I noticed it was Dresser's picture on the T-shirts. I was told he had killed himself. I was sad. I must admit I had felt a little safer knowing he was hanging around and hearing him say "Pretty Girl", and now he was gone, just like that.

I remember being at Kennedy-King we were about to go on Spring Break. A classmate of mine told me how she was going to Atlanta. She wasn't going to make her oldest son go with her this time. We talked about her moving out the neighborhood, because she felt if she didn't her son would be led down the wrong path. Spring Break came and went. After school resumed, I attended the class that she and I had together, and she got up to make her presentation.

She talked about violence and the crime rate; she also mentioned that her son had been killed during Spring Break. I went numb. I wondered how she was even able to come to class and make that speech. I spoke with her after class and she told me what happened. The boy that I had seen on the news found shot in the head was her son. ***Teen Found in Dumpster One Of Three Mourned***, is what the March 14, 2008 headline read. She didn't even know he was dead until she came back from Atlanta. Her son was staying with a cousin while she was away, and the cousin just thought the boy had run off, he was only thirteen. He was shot and stuffed in a trash can by our apartment. Many things happened in Englewood, but those two events stick out to me the most, because they hit close to home. A guy who I didn't know had saved my life then took his own life and a friend whose worse fears came true. I had been in Englewood for two years and had seen more than enough to run away, but I didn't. Lois and I really weren't able to leave. The apartment was all we could afford, and many people didn't take a chance on us because we lacked good credit. We stayed because we had to, and we made the best of it.

Keep Ya Head Up

I continued working for Mrs. Howard and going to school. The money from financial aid helped me. I had extra money for bills, other necessities, and to pay Chicago State. I hadn't forgot about that. Lois had gotten a part-time job at a hospital. It seemed like things were fine for once. We eventually bought more furniture and those headboards from Ashraf. Bernita still came around and stayed with us on the weekends. One day, Bernita was staying the night and my friend Nick was over there. Nick said that she looked pregnant; we laughed it off. A few months later Bernita called and told me she was six months pregnant. I was shocked and concerned. Bernita's situation wasn't much better than mine, I was wondering how she would care for the baby. We had a baby shower for Bernita. One day Bernita's mom called and said she was in labor. Lois and I rushed to the hospital. We didn't make it in time, but we made it before she named him. Bernita couldn't think of a name. She wanted a name that started with a D, Lois came up with the name Devin. That is how my god son got the name.

Bernita started looking for work as soon as she had the baby. She had a cousin that worked at a call center. Her cousin suggested that she apply, and she suggested that I apply. Once again, Bernita and I went for an interview and test on the same day. We passed both and were offered employment. It was a part-time telemarketing job. I was still working for Mrs. Howard, but the pay caring for her was only $7.50, and I was only working three hours a day. I would be making $9.00 hourly during the week and getting at least six hours a day at this new job. It was a no brainer, I was out. Mrs. Howard was heartbroken that I was leaving. We had formed a bond, and I really did care about and her family. I promised that I would continue to visit, and I did for a while. But with increased working hours and school demands, the visits eventually stopped. I think about her today and wonder if she is alive. She had a good heart.

Bernita and I started working at the call center. We worked overtime when we could and were never absent. I felt good making more money. We were paid $11.00 when we worked overtime and got good quality scores. The job wasn't hard at all. We had to call customers and conduct surveys about the service they received from various companies. The point was completing the most surveys with the customers and typing notes verbatim in the shortest amount of time. Many times, the customers hung up on us, most of the time you could only get them to complete the short surveys. Bernita and I were top performers.

Me Against the World

My grandfather had agreed to still pay my phone bill. One day, when Bernita and I were getting off work, I discovered that my phone was off. I called my grandfather, and he said that he wasn't paying the bill anymore. I told him ok. Bernita and I went to a phone store down the street and we both bought new phones. (I was disappointed that my grandfather didn't even give me a warning, but I refused to argue about it I just did what I had to do.) I wasn't surprised by anything.

I then felt like the only people I could trust and depend on were Arnetta, my grandmother and Mr. Ruben, and soon enough even that changed. I called Mr. Ruben for help. I was working and making more money, but sometimes I would still get behind. I called Mr. Ruben and explained my situation to him. Mr. Ruben had helped me since high school, so I felt comfortable asking him for help. When I asked this time, Mr. Ruben said the he had something to talk to me about. I told him to go ahead, start talking.

Mr. Ruben started talking about how he started looking at me as a woman once I was eighteen and how he had developed these romantic feelings towards me! He talked about a time when were in the mall and I had on an outfit that he remembered. He talked about how my legs and breasts looked in the outfit. He talked about how it was hard to resist an urge he had that day. I stopped him immediately and cursed him out and told him to never call me again. My world was shattered. I couldn't believe that the man I looked up to, had spent so much time with, really was who everybody said he was, a pervert. He had been grooming me, waiting until he had the chance to make his move. Everything that he had done for me or taught me was with bad intentions. I felt so disappointed and hurt. I had defended him against people that said he was a pervert, my own grandmother questioned his intentions, and I never saw it coming. I never spoke to him again and I never told my mom, because I knew she would kill him. I never told anybody until now. Mr. Ruben died almost two years ago. I tried to make it to the funeral, but my car broke down. I felt like I still should have paid my respects, even though I never wanted to see or hear from him again.

Play Your Cards Right

I had started making decent money at the new job, so I decided that it was time to get my own place. Lois and I had lived together for more than two years. We hadn't had a fight or argument. I just wanted my own place. I mentioned to Lois that I would be moving, and she said that was fine. She knew another friend from school that would need a place to stay soon. Months went by, and an apartment became available next door to our apartment in the same building. I thought it would be an easy move, so I set my eye on that apartment. In all honesty, I wanted to remain close by so I could look out for Lois; sometimes I thought she was too nice for her own good. I called the apartment office and they informed me that since Lois and I were such good tenants, I wouldn't have to pay a deposit or the full amount to move in. I was excited about that news.

Months later, and Bernita and I started hearing about a new job everybody was leaving our current job to take. We heard the job was paying $15.00 an hour and looking for people with telemarketing skills. We wanted to know more about this. So, I asked a colleague on the current job about it. She had applied and interviewed the next day, and the job was offered. The job was located at Colorado Technical University (CTU). They wanted people that could make hundreds of outbound calls daily and had good customer service skills. Bernita and I figured we could do this. Bernita and I applied and were interviewed on the same day.

We were offered employment a few days later. I was so happy. I had never made that much money before. During that time, $15.00 hourly was a lot to a person without children. I knew I was really going to move out now. More money and more time for school was huge for me. The only dilemma was that this part-time job was considered temporary. I didn't want to leave my permanent job for something temporary. The other dilemma was that I would have to change my school schedule again. I would have to go to school in the mornings and work during the evenings. I hated working evenings, but I took the job anyway.

We started the job. I would be coming in, and Bernita would be going out. The job was easy. We had to reach out to prospective students to see if they wanted more information about the university or if they wanted to speak to an advisor. We mad about 500 calls daily. I liked the comfortable environment and sitting at a computer all day. The more I worked and calculated ore what I was bringing in, the more I planned to get my own place. I started buying things for my new place and keeping them in my room at my current apartment. I bought my first living room set for $400 from some other Arabs we knew. The set was black leather. I kept it in my room wrapped in plastic, waiting for my move. I wasn't about to move into my first apartment without anything again. I then called the leasing office to see if the apartment was still available and they said yes.

In our neighborhood there weren't many stores around; everything was on 71st and State. We lived on 68th street. I was relived to find out we had a few stores on the corner by our house. The small strip had a convenience store, a dentist, and a restaurant. All the students at Kennedy-King and I went to the convenience store regularly. I found out that all the businesses were owned by the same person, a man called Smooth. He was an old retired. Smooth was also in the drug and gambling business and a loan shark. He was the type that thought he was still young and cool. I thought the fact that he still wore cornrows was hilarious. The more I went to the store, the more we talked. We talked about our families, where we were from, and the neighborhood. He liked to talk about his past a lot; I just listened to be nice.

Smooth started giving me things for free and hinting around how he could take care of me. I tried to ignore him, he was married, and his daughter worked in the shop. The more I ignored him, the more he flirted. I then started thinking Why not use this situation to my advantage. I started getting everything for free from all the stores. I never kissed him, but he had my phone number and that was enough. A lady named Rose worked in the store with Smooth most of the time, and she and I were cool. Rose had lost her husband and children in a house fire. She also had a history of drug use. We would all have a good time talking and reminiscing. I think Rose suspected something was going on between Smooth and me, but she never said it.

    I was dating other guys while still leading Smooth on. One day I was on a date, and my tooth started hurting. I had been having toothaches off and on but never like this. I had to ask my date to take me home because I was in so much pain. I tried everything to get rid of that toothache. I was without insurance, so I couldn't just go to the dentist and get it checked. I bought kits from the store and tried home remedies. I went to work in pain for weeks. I knew Smooth owned a dentist office, but I rarely saw a dentist there. I asked him about the dentist, and he said he could get him to come to look at my tooth. I told him I couldn't pay for it. He told me not to worry about it. The dentist came, but he couldn't pull the tooth because the roots were too big. He said I would need an oral surgeon. I knew I couldn't afford an oral surgeon either, but Smooth said he knew one that I could visit. I told him I only had the money to move into my apartment that I had saved, so I couldn't afford an oral surgeon. Smooth told me he would pay the cost, but I would have to pay the interest. I told him that was fine. I was desperate. I needed that tooth removed.

The day that I the appointment to get the tooth removed, was the same day that I was supposed to move into my apartment. I didn't care. I had the tooth pulled that morning. The cost was $300, so I had to pay Smooth $450. Tim, my friend from Chicago State and I started moving my stuff from one apartment to the next. I told him I wanted to be done before the numbness in my tooth wore off, and we got it done. Once I moved in, Smooth gave me some brand-new black tables to go with my living-room set. I had my bedroom set and TV from the apartment Lois and I had. I also bought a card table with four chairs for the living room. I was proud of my first apartment. I felt so at peace that first night.

My next two checks went to Smooth; I wanted to make sure I paid him back, so he wouldn't ask for anything in return. After paying him back, he knew I was trustworthy. He started giving me all kinds of money that I didn't have to pay back. I would call Tim and ask him to take me shopping for my new place almost every weekend. He didn't mind because I gave him gas money. I felt bad leading Smooth on, but not too bad, because he was sweet on many women around the neighborhood. He told me he liked me because I was strong-minded and feisty. I think he liked when I talked crazy to him. At this time, my uncle George moved out of his apartment, so he gave me more stuff for my place. I had comforter sets, pictures, rugs, towels, a microwave, and a marble kitchen table set all for free. My friends would come to my house and be like how are you able to afford this stuff? They couldn't believe I was living on my own in Englewood in an apartment that was so nice.

Troublesome

Here comes a situation that I'm not too proud about. I walked into Smooth's store one day after class, and there wasn't anyone up front. I would always stop by between classes or after classes for snacks or just to talk. I yelled his name and didn't get an answer, so I walked to his office in the back. His car was out front, so I knew he was there. I had never been in the back before. Once there, I found Smooth sleep at his desk. I startled him out of his sleep he grinned and said, "you done caught me slipping." I laughed and nodded nervously, because I was trying to make sense of what I was seeing. All around the office, wall to wall was cocaine. Cocaine so white it was achromatic. The light reflected off the cocaine and blurred my vison. It looked like compacted flour. Each row neatly laid and stacked on one another. Smooth realized what I was looking at and said, "what you thinking about" I said "you dumb to be back here sleep knowing you got all this back here," He laughed and said, "Even playas slip sometimes" He then asked if I knew what it was, and I said "of course I did I'm not dumb"

He said, "I'm actually glad you had a chance to see this," I asked him why, and he said because he had been meaning to run something past me. Smooth told me he thought I was a strong- minded young woman with a good head on her shoulders who could use some help. Buttering me up of course, but I bought it. I thought he was about to start in about us getting together again, and I was prepared to shut him down again. He then asked if I would be interested in a business opportunity, I told him yes. I had spent the past two years trying not to become a product of my environment. I didn't get involved with any dudes from the neighborhood, had not befriended females from Englewood, and I had also avoided the drug business.

Smooth laid out the business opportunity. It involved me taking some risks but the money I could make made it all seem worthwhile. I had just moved into a new apartment, and trying to pay Chicago State back, I was also trying to make sure my mom was straight. seemed like an opportunity I couldn't pass up. I guess you can say I did become a product of my environment eventually. I would have never got involved in something like this back home. I was from a place where everybody knew everybody, and you couldn't trust anybody. I was an adult, living in the hood, with a whole lot of weight on my shoulders. The decision wasn't hard. Smooth would give me an ounce of cocaine worth $1000 dollars to sell.

He said if I could "get it off" then I could keep half. The rest would go to him. I told him I didn't know enough people to even think about selling drugs. He told me to go look outside across the street, so I did and came back. He said "What did you see" I said "The school" he smiled and said "Exactly," "This is Englewood; you don't think out of all those people at the school or in this neighborhood ain't nobody doing drugs? I told him I'm sure there are some people on drugs. hell, I even listened to people in class talk about their past drug addictions, but what does that have to do with me? He said, "Don't you get it, it would work out perfect for you. You already go to school there and you don't have to worry about trafficking." I told him I wasn't down with all that. No way would I risk getting caught selling drugs on school grounds. I told him to give me the stuff. I would find my own way to "get it off". He smiled and said, "Alright boss'

I put the stuff in my backpack in between my books and walked home through the alley. I rushed through my back door and threw the backpack onto the kitchen table. I had to get my thoughts together. I had an adrenalin rush; I couldn't believe what I had just done. I thought about taking it right back to him, but then I didn't want to seem like a punk. I kept telling myself to be cool and think. I needed somebody that I could trust to help me. The problem was everybody I trusted lived six hours away. A light bulb went off in my head: Nick was the person I should call. I knew I could trust him. He would know how to get rid of the stuff. I called him up and told him to stop by my apartment when he got off work. Nick stopped by and was like, "what's up" "somebody did something to you? I was like, Naw. "I have to show you something." I went in the kitchen, went under the cabinet, and showed it to him Nick said, "Where the hell you get that from"? I was like don't worry about it; can you get it off? He said, "hell yeah" "what's the move though?" I told him I had to give half to the person I got it from, and I could keep the other half. Nick said, "That don't make sense. How much did you pay for it? I told him I didn't pay anything. He burst out laughing and said, "One of your lame-ass Vicks must have given it to you." We both started laughing and came up with a plan. I told Nick I would give him $200 of my $500, I wasn't tripping because it did not cost me anything in the first place.

One week later I walked into Smooth's store and told him I had something for him. Grinning, He told me to walk to the back. Rose and Smooth's daughter just looked each other with knowing glances. Once in the back I put his money on the table. He asked how did I do it? I told him, "I have my ways" I never told him about Nick, and I never told Nick about Smooth. The $300 was cool and all, but I wanted more, I always told myself if I was going to do something like this, I was going to do it all the way. Smooth was more than willing to continue doing business with me and at a discounted price. I had hit a sweet lick as they say. The only catch was that I couldn't get it for free, so this new job would help. I continued working at the school, getting paid every week, and re-copping with Smooth. I wasn't a fool though; I got an extra bank account and saved every chance that I could. I didn't plan on doing it forever, and to be honest, I really didn't have time between work and school.

Nick got caught slipping a few times, and I had to bail him out jail, I felt it was only right because in all actuality, he was really the one taking the risk. I got the drugs from Smooth, gave them to Nick, and Nick got the money to me. One-night Nick called me from the back of the paddy wagon. He had gotten arrested for a DUI. I got on the train, headed out West, and bailed him out. Nick had always been there for me since day one and I tried to be there for him. I never told anybody what we had going on.

My mom said she wanted to go back to school and get her GED. I said cool. I would pay the bills she had, and she could go back to school. She never questioned where I was getting the money from. I was buying her furniture, designer clothes, bags, and anything else she wanted, So, imagine my surprise when I found out she had quit the GED program without telling me. I was so mad. I felt like here, I am taking risks and chances trying to look out for you and you lie and deceive me? I never stopped doing things for her though, but I refused to pay her bills anymore. She was going to have to get a job.

The crazy thing is that everybody started joking about me selling drugs but never really thought it. I would buy something for my house with cash and

Tim would be like "You must be selling drugs." I would laugh and say, "yea right how and when?" My co-workers would come over, and they would ask "how are you able to afford this on what we make? I always told them I was a good saver and good at budgeting, which was true. The system Nick and I had continued, and before I knew it, I had been at my job at CTU for a year. I was a top performer at CTU. I received peer qualifier of the month every month, and eventually I received peer qualifier of the year. I was moved to another team because another supervisor wanted me on his team. The other team members didn't want me on their team, so they trashed my desk. They tore up my certificates and threw my plaque in the trash. I reported it, but nothing was ever done.

I eventually became close with this girl named Tanisha. She was a short thick girl from Atlanta. Everybody thought we looked alike and asked if we were sisters. Tanisha was a sweetheart. We went to clubs together, met guys together, and did each other's hair. We remain friends to this day.

I remember one-time Tanisha and I was at Lois apartment when we heard the alarm go off on Tanisha car. We ran downstairs; I had my pistol with me. We only saw one person saying that someone had bumped her car and made the alarm go off, we didn't see any windows broken or anything, so we didn't know what to believe. Tanisha couldn't stop laughing at me running downstairs with that gun. A couple of years in Englewood and my new line of business made me never hesitate to have the strap on me. Tanisha had also speculated that I had something illegal going on but never said anything. One time we went on a shopping spree, I was buying designer bags, clothes, shoes etc, I spent so much money that I had to call the bank, so they could increase my spending limit on my account. I told Tanisha that I had gotten some scholarship money. I had a good thing going and I wasn't about to ruin it by running my mouth.

Nick and I still had our thing going, and we were making good money. It was all good because I only trusted him, and he only trusted me. Like all good things, this good thing came to an end. We did most of our business on the Westside, so I went out there a lot sometimes for business and sometimes just to hang. Bernita lived out West too, so between she and Nick I was out there on the regular.

Death Around the Corner

I counted five shots; I was covered in blood. I couldn't hear anything after the shots. I didn't know if he was dead or alive, had I been shot? Where was everybody else? Was I dead? These were questions I asked myself while on my back on a bathroom floor of a pool hall. A body was on top of me. I suddenly heard the police and paramedics screaming, "ma'am are you shot? Can you hear us?" I could hear them, but they sounded so far away. I was in a daze it's like they were moving in slow motion. I watched them push Red over and start examining him to see where he was shot and if he was living or dead.

A cop finally pulled me up from the floor. I stood on my two feet and came back to reality. "We need you to come with us to the station" "We need you to tell us what happened" I just nodded my head slowly and obliged. I sat in the police station five hours telling them the same thing repeatedly. I didn't know what happened. I couldn't identify the shooter if I saw him. I didn't know the victim. I told them I came downstairs to see a friend and hang out. My friend left, and I went to use the bathroom. Before I left, a guy ran in and another guy was behind him, and he started shooting. That was my story and I was sticking to it, but it was not true. How did I end up in this situation?

This is what really happened. One night I was bored, so I called Nick and told him I was coming to see him, he said cool just let him know when I was getting off the train because he was at the pool hall downstairs from his apartment. When I arrived at the pool hall, I saw Nick talking to this dude, Red, that liked me. We all chatted, Red asked me if I wanted a drink, and I told him yes. Red came back with the drink and we stood by the pool table talking and drinking. The pool hall was packed, but I could still watch my surroundings. A guy walked up to Red and asked can he use the pool table, Red told him go ahead, because we weren't using it anyway. Red and I kept talking never giving the guy another thought. The guy and his friend finished playing pool and left. Me and Red had been dancing and laughing messing with Nick. Nick did not want me talking to Red.

We never noticed the guy and his friend come back into the pool hall. I saw one of the guys look at Red and me nod his head. In a split-second shots rang out. Red dragged me backwards into the bathroom. He then laid his body kind of across my lap but halfway sitting up with his head almost on top of mine. Red kept saying, "Be quiet" "Don't scream" I didn't scream but I was crying, and scared. Red kept telling me to be quiet, but I couldn't stop crying. Then the room got quiet and I thought it was over, but the bathroom door crept open and one of the shooters was standing in the doorway. He looked at Red and fired five shots and quickly ran off. I was too scared to come out the bathroom, but I couldn't stand just sit there with all the blood on me. I then started daydreaming. My life really flashed before my eyes. I thought "Damn how did I end up in this?" I should have stayed out South.

I couldn't sleep that night because I kept thinking about Red. Was, he dead? Would the shooter try to come find me because he knows that I saw his face? And what the hell had happened to Nick? I finally drifted off to sleep. The next morning, I immediately called Nick, but his phone kept going to voicemail, I called a few of his other friends and didn't get an answer. I thought, "It's not like Nick to not get in touch with me after something like this has happened. I thought maybe he was dead. I even thought maybe he had set Red up. Days and weeks went by and I didn't hear from or see Nick. I started getting worried about Nick because I know Nick wouldn't just disappear. One day as I was leaving work, I noticed I had a voicemail; it was Nick's mom asking me to call her. She had gotten my number from my stepdad, who was a deacon at her husband's church. Nick had told her to contact me. She told me Nick was in jail. He had been caught by the police chasing one of the shooters; he had been arrested and charged with possession of marijuana and a firearm.

Nick already had a record, so he was facing some time. I gave his mother my address, so he can write me. Nick finally called and wrote, and I told him I would help him get out of jail. Nick told me he had been praying for me every night. He said he hoped I was safe. I used some of my money I had saved up to get Nick an attorney and he took care of the rest. Nick had to do a few months in jail and the rest in boot camp. He also told me Red had lived. I know it seems cold, but I was not thinking about Red! On one hand he had saved my life and on the other he was a man that somebody wanted dead. I never wanted to see Red again. I never found out the whole story behind everything that happened that night and I honestly didn't want to know. I was glad to be alive; God had spared me for the second time.

I was glad everything worked out for Nick and that I was alive, but I still had a dilemma. I still had product to sell. I decided then to tell Smooth that I wasn't doing it anymore and just give the stuff back to him. I was new to the game, so I didn't know that you just can't give the product back and say you aren't selling anymore; it doesn't work like that. I kept contemplating about what to do. I would take the alley home from school just to avoid walking by the store and seeing Smooth. I let a couple of weeks go by, and finally I was just thought "Forget it, let me call Smooth and tell him what's up. I called for days, no answer. I walked to the store. It was locked up and nobody was there. I didn't know what to do. One day I was leaving Walgreens, and I saw Rose. She yelled my name and ran over to me. I asked her what was up with Smooth and she told me somebody had broken into his house and shot him.

The doctors said Smooth would never walk again. Rose said she had been looking for me and had even come to my apartment, but I wasn't home. I told her to tell Smooth I hope he got better. I didn't call or try to go see him either because he was married, and I had no idea what to say or how to explain our relationship.

One day out of the blue I was leaving school and I saw Smooth car at the store. I went in and there he was in a wheelchair, smiling with that gold tooth shining. I hugged him and talked about everything that had happened over the last few months. I told him I didn't want to keep doing what we were doing because my friend wouldn't be able to help anymore. Smooth looked at me and said, "So you gone let another motherfucker stop your money"? "look at me, they tried to take me out, but I ain't letting that stop my hustle." I said "naw, but I don't really have a choice. "How else am I going get it off?" I had too much going for myself to be selling. Smooth just smiled and said" I know a way"

I'm not going to lie; I was used to the extra money outside of my work check. In Chicago, the cost of living was so high. On top of that I had people to look after: my mom, my godson and whoever else I helped at the time. I had almost been killed; Nick was in jail, and Smooth was paralyzed. It seemed like those three reasons would be enough to get out the game, but they weren't.

I had set some expensive goals for myself. I needed to pay Chicago State off before I graduated, and I needed a certain amount of money saved up for Law School, because I knew I could not work full time and be a Law student. I'm not making excuses as to why I did what I did. I know a lot of people will say there were million other things that I could have done for extra money, but, I had already tried them all. I almost tried stripping, and grunt work, I was tired of struggling. I look back now and realize I was selfish and had tunnel vision. I didn't think that my freedom was worth more than comfort. I didn't realize that all the things I hoped to gain could have been taken away by a bullet or a jail cell in an instant. I was young and determined to get what I wanted by any means necessary. Never say what you will or won't do. You never know what you would do until you are faced with reality.

Shorty Wanna Be a Thug

Money is not the root of all evil. What's evil are the things you do to get money. The fact that you make yourself believe that you need it even when you don't. Nick was released from jail and I caught him up to speed on everything. While he was locked up, we did not discuss anything that happened, because we knew calls were recorded and letters read. I told Nick I was flying straight, and that Smooth wasn't in the drug business anymore either because of the incident that had left him paralyzed. But I was lying. I told myself once I had a certain amount saved up and graduated from Kennedy-King, I was done. To be done in that time and to get the money saved up, I needed all profit. So, I cut Nick out. I figured with the plan Smooth and I had come up with, I didn't need a middleman. I had enough nerves to do everything on my own. Nick had his own thing going. Our thing was just extra. I wasn't taking money out of his hands, but the fact that I lied, was wrong.

One thing about Karma is that it always comes back. Smooth knew I was still not that comfortable with dealing with people face-to-face, so he hooked me up with his nephew, Dre. I messed up right there. I never do things with people I don't know. I did this time though, because I trusted Smooth and I counted on his nephew's loyalty to him for protection. One night I was in my apartment watching TV, and I heard a knock on my door. It was strange because I lived on the third floor, and we had to buzz people up. Nobody came over to my place without calling. I answered the door and there was a young girl asking if I had a phone she could use. I rudely told her no and shut the door. I heard another knock, and this time she asked if I needed some food stamps. By now, my antennas were up. Did somebody send her? Was she casing my spot? I told her to wait a minute and went to get my pistol. When I went back to the door she was running down the stairs. I chased after her and ran right into the police. They were in the building because of a domestic issue. I was scared to death. The officer asked what was going on, and I told him some kids had been playing at my door. I don't know where the girl disappeared to. I was on edge after that. I was always bringing in shopping bags or having furniture delivered, so I'm sure someone started noticed. I had a guy I was dealing with at the time and he lived in another city. I told him I was getting scared living by myself in that neighborhood. I didn't tell him the real reason why I was scared and paranoid.

He offered to pay for an alarm system on my apartment. I felt better after the alarm system was installed.

I was a month away from graduation and living the life. I had a nice amount in the bank, my CTU friends and I were hanging out all the time, especially Tanish and me. I told myself time was ticking though, so I had to stop the spending and buckle down. I said I was done with the sideline gig after graduation. I had reached my desired amount. Graduation was on my mother's birthday, which was also Mother's Day. I chose not to attend graduation and to go visit her instead. I bought her lavish gifts, gave her money, and she never suspected a thing. I regret not attending my graduation. To me, it was just a means to an end, a necessary step to the bigger goal. I was at the top of the graduation class, and had become a faculty favorite, but none of that mattered. I was caught up in getting money and trying to race to the finish line. My Associate's Degree mean the most to me. I went through the most to get it, and it defined my coming-of-age period.

I had made a year at CTU before I started hearing about a job at another school. I was all about money, so I got the information and applied. I was a shoo-in because I had just gotten my degree, and my track record at CTU was very good. I went for the job and was hired the same day. I had one issue, though. Now that I had paid Chicago State their $7000 back, I was able to register for school and even had a schedule. My school schedule and the new job schedule conflicted. So, I was faced with making another decision. I was stuck between staying at my part-time job without any benefits and finishing up my last year and a half at Chicago State, or taking the job and putting school off.

I chose the job. I had never had a job making such good money, and I told myself the money would help me get out "The game." I said the sideline situation didn't control me or change me, but it did. It became the deciding factor in my decisions. It took up most of my time. It changed my attitude. It changed me. I started the job, and after six months I decided two things, one was that I could still get my Bachelors' degree at the school I worked for. It was accredited, and they would help pay for it. The schedule was flexible, and all my credits transferred from Kennedy-King and Chicago State, so it really would only take a year and a half to complete. Secondly, I was done with the sideline gig; at this point I was leasing apartments with Ashraf and working my new job. The school was paid off, so I really didn't need to do it anymore. I was done but not before one last time.

I called Dre, Smooth's nephew and told him this was going to be last time. I was going to bring him what I had, and he could just pay me for it and do whatever he wanted. Dre texted me the address, and I told him I would be heading out in about fifteen minutes. The address wasn't far from my house; I jumped on the L, took a bus and then walked to the apartment building. I had a strange feeling come over me, but I figured it was because I was cautious about the neighborhood. I called Dre, but he didn't pick up. I then sent him a text and he told me to ring the bell so he could buzz me up. I rang the bell and walked up to the apartment. The door was open, so I walked in. Two dudes were sitting at a card table, but neither one of them was Dre. "Where is Dre?" I asked, the dude with the stocking cap on replied, "Oh he tied up right now" and they both start laughing. I could feel something was off. "He just texted me, so how he is all of sudden tied up?" I asked. "Bitch you asking too many questions; don't you have something for us?" Dude with the stocking cap on said. I told him I didn't have anything for him. He stood up and got closer to the door where I was standing. "Dre ain't who texted you" he said. I knew then it was a set up or something. His friend got up, but he went to the bedroom for something. I thought he was coming towards me. I told him I didn't know what was going on. He could have the shit, just let me go. He said "Naw baby girl, we are keeping you so you can call Dre's uncle" I told them I didn't know Dre's uncle.

He said I was lying. I told him I swear I didn't, my boyfriend sent me there. He slapped me so hard my lips felt like they were swollen. I didn't even think twice before my blade was out. I stabbed him in the shoulder and just kept stabbing I had such an adrenalin rush that I couldn't stop. His friend heard him yelling and came out, and he had a smirk on his face. The smirk turned to shock and as soon as he said, "What the fuck" my gun was out. I always carried both; I figured if I could stab someone and get out of a situation, I would rather do that than shoot them. The friend saw my gun and said "oh shit. "Shorty strapped" I told him, "Don't come close to me or I would shoot him. He came closer anyway. My hands were sweating, and my heart was beating fast. I had been to a gun range before. I had written a paper on how to shoot someone in self-defense. I had never shot a real target before. I pictured what the headline would read if I was killed here. *"Young girl killed in what appeared to be an attempted robbery* "I had never shot to kill or injure anyone before, and I was hoping it just scared him. I knew I only had a few seconds to decide. I closed my eyes and fired the gun. I heard a scream, but I couldn't tell if it was him or his friend that was one the floor. I dropped the package and ran down two flights of steps. It was a bus stop right in front of the building, but I ran two stops away. I had my backpack on with the gun in it, but I had left the knife. I was scared, out of breath and praying the bus came soon. I kept hearing sirens, but they were going in other directions. The bus finally came, and I was so out of it I almost missed my stop. I jumped on the L and got off at 69th street, but I didn't go straight home, because I didn't know if somebody may have been following or chasing me. I waited at the McDonalds trying to get myself together. I was calling Smooth repeatedly and he was not picking up. I would have sat there forever if an African man hadn't brought to my attention that I had blood on me. I didn't even realize it. I had taken the bus and the L with blood on me and not even one person said anything.

I walked home fast and flew up those three flights of stairs. I had to get out of my clothes and shower. I got out of the shower, changed clothes, and just sat on my living room floor with my legs crossed Indian style. I couldn't get myself together. Finally, my phone rang. It was Smooth. He told me to meet him at the store in twenty minutes. I was scared to leave back out, and I didn't trust him either, so I grabbed my gun and headed out the backdoor. I met Smooth at the store, and he already knew what had happened in fact, he had a picture to go with the story. Bottom line: Dre was dead because of Smooth and I was going to be collateral damage if it had been up to them.

I was out. I was done. I had been spared for the 3rd time. I could possibly have murdered two people. In Chicago, people get stabbed and shot every day, and the police take forever to get to the "hood", even if somebody heard the shot, they wouldn't have done anything. The other thing is that if the dudes weren't dead it was unlikely that they would call the cops and tell them they had planned to kidnap a girl, but she stabbed and shot them instead. I really shouldn't have feared going to jail, but I did. I then buried myself in school and work to keep my mind off of it, but I was always looking over my shoulder, and I never left my apartment without my gun. As for Smooth, I felt bad because of the loss of his nephew, but whatever friendship we had came to an end. I had gotten out alive. I wasn't dumb enough to go back.

Toss It Up

With this craziness going on, I needed a vacation. I had never even been on a vacation as an adult, So, I called Arnetta, Amanda, and my best friend Renee and we made plans to visit Miami. At the time, I was making the most money of us four, on top of what I had saved, so I paid for the entire trip. and told them they could pay me back. I was excited and looking forward to doing something normal and to be around some familiar faces. We planned the trip for June. The trip was difficult to schedule, because I had been at my job for less than a year, so I didn't have any vacation days. Somehow it all worked out, and we agreed on a weekend vacation in June.

I met up with Arnetta and Amanda in St Louis, and we all flew out together. Renee was flying in from Georgia, so she was meeting us in Miami. We were supposed to arrive in Miami at about 2:30, but we arrived at 1 am. A series of things happened that caused such a huge delay. As soon as we boarded the plane, the pilot told everyone to get off immediately! We got off. The back of the plane had caught on fire. We were scared; we even considered not going at all. After about 90 minutes, another plane arrived, and we resumed our trip.

Once we boarded this plane and was settled in, the pilot explained some other issues that were going on, so we sat for another hour. Finally, the plane took off, and we arrived in Miami. It was storming heavily, and, to top it off we didn't have anywhere to land. So, we had to stay in the air for another 45 minutes until they found somewhere for us to land. Once we landed, we started looking for the car-rental area. When we got there, we encountered more problems. By this time, we were pretty sure we were being punked. We exchanged some nasty words with the car rental associate, and before I knew it, the cops were called, and they put us out. It was almost 2 am, and most of the transportation companies had stopped running. We had no idea how we were going to get to our hotel.

Finally, a guy in a cab pulled up and asked if we needed a ride. We said yeah and jumped in. We were exhausted and ready to get to the hotel. The driver's English was not very good, but we did make out that he said he was going to take us to another car rental place. He pulled off, and sped up, but he wasn't going towards the highway. It seemed he was going through a wooded area. We also could hear him on the phone saying, "Yes, I have four of them" instantly our radars went off! We had watched enough movies to know something was up. I pulled out the knife I had, and Arnetta had hers as well. We told him we wanted to go to our hotel. We had already prepared ourselves to take him down if he made any moves! Luckily for us and him, he did get back on the highway and get us to our hotel.

Then we faced even more problems when we arrived at that hotel. The hotel manager told us that the room we reserved had flooded. They did not have any more rooms, so we had to stay at a hotel a couple two blocks away. Blocks in Miami are long, So, imagine us, tired, frustrated, and disgusted walking down the street with our luggage. Finally, we made it to the hotel, and I swear, it seemed like the hotel from the *The Shining*. The hotel seemed deserted; we didn't see any other guests but us. The bell hop told us that they practiced "quiet hours" but, that was not a rule we were going to follow. We were going to do what we wanted. We got to the room, and it was even worse, small and dingy. We decided that even though it was late, and we had been through hell to get there, we still were going to make the best of it. It was Miami, so we were sure we could find something to get into. We got dressed and thought we were about to head out.

Then the door wouldn't open. No matter how we pushed and pulled, it would not work. We were locked inside the room. We immediately called the front desk and the bell hop who spoke broken English said he would be down to help us. He did come with a toolbox, but he just sat it down and never came back. We were so mad! We could even see some Mexican people outside our door trying to peek in, but not trying to help. The room was hot and stuffy, and there were no windows. Finally, Arnetta bust the door down! We were determined to get out of that room. We could not wait to give the bellhop a piece of our mind. The only thing he did was apologize, at least that was the only thing we could make out that he said. We still went out.

We found a little shabby bar that was open. It had music and liquor, which was all we needed. We threw back Patron shot after Patron shot. We made ourselves have a good time. Arnetta and Renee went back to the room early, while Amanda and I stayed. Pretty soon, we were getting free patron shots! We were having a blast, until the bartender offered us some cocaine. That was our cue to get up out of there; we were party girls, but not those kinds of party girls. The next day we demanded our reserved rooms. So, the next morning there we were again, walking luggage down the street to the hotel we were originally supposed to stay.

The trip began to be fun. We had a much nicer room and a fresh start on a new day. We shopped, partied, and took tours. We even made friends with some professional boxers that were staying at our hotel. They became part of the group during our trip and went everywhere with us. We went to the hippest clubs and had plenty more shots, including body shots. We danced the night away until five in the morning.

Thug Passion

Were there men in my life? Absolutely. It took me a while to jump into the dating scene when I moved to Chicago. I was caught between three lovers, one was my high school sweetheart, one was in Iraq, and the other one was back home trying to get into law school. The first-year I was juggling all three long-distance relationships and keeping the lines of communication open with two men in jail. I preferred it this way, because I didn't have to be available for one man all the time. I only had to call, email, IM, or write letters and that was fine with me.

Eventually, someone caught my eye, and I was determined that he was going to be the one that helped me get my feet wet in Chicago. He was tall, caramel complexioned, and quiet. The initial attraction was that he reminded me of my high school sweetheart. I later found out they were nothing alike. I made it known that I was interested, and we flirted for a while. I knew that it couldn't be anything serious because I had heard that he had just broken up with his girlfriend. Eventually he called me, and I went to see him. It was late, so the security guard was giving me the side eye, but I didn't care. She didn't know me. He didn't have a roommate, so that was perfect. We did what we did, but I made it clear that nothing else would happen and he was cool with that. We were too cool with it, because that situation lasted until I moved from Chicago. Who has a "dip" for six years? This girl. After he moved out of the dorms, and he would still pick me up. I would stay at his apartment and sneak back to the dorms in the morning. Once I moved out, he started coming to the apartment I shared with Lois almost every weekend. We kept that up until I moved into my own apartment, and he came there frequently. Did we eventually start feeling like more than dips? Yes. Did we ever act on it? No. We didn't let any of our friends know we were dealing with each other and nor did we go out on dates. We had arguments and several break ups, but I remained clear about what I wanted. While I was dealing with him, I had been on and off with the guy that lived in the other city, and in love with a man serving in Iraq. I was still writing my incarcerated friends, promising them loyalty, knowing I didn't have any real intentions for them. I was young and exercising my free will.

A young, single woman living in the city. Can have a very interesting sex life. I will always remember the story about Penectomy. That was what I called a guy that I once dated. Penectomy was fine! He had a perfect body, was a gentleman. He was also a doctor and a part-time professor at Kennedy-King. He had all these excellent qualities, but he was single. I should have taken that as a warning sign, but my ego made believe I just had it going on. Penectomy took me out all the time. We went to plays, movies, and all the finest restaurants. He bought me clothes and real designer bags. I found out I didn't like sushi or caviar from going out with Penectomy. I felt like we could potentially be something, but we hadn't had sex yet. I held out because I didn't want to rush things. He was so fine I knew once I turned loose there would be no turning back.

Finally, the time came for us to become intimate. His foreplay was superb! It seemed to go on forever. I eventually let him know I was ready. He grabbed a condom, and even though the lights were off I could hear that he was having a hard time. I kept hearing a strange noise. I turned on the light and saw something I had never seen in my entire life. Penectomy was small, and not regular small, but birth-defect small. I was totally freaked out, so I had to think fast and faked a headache. I couldn't put him out quickly enough! As soon as he left, I went into the kitchen got on my computer, and researched what I had just seen. I called my friend, Tanisha, and told her I thought he had a penectomy procedure. I didn't want him to think it was all about sex, so I went out with him a few more times. I knew in the back of my mind that he was going to try again, and I would have to shut him down. Sure enough, he did, but this time he was aggressive, almost like a rapist. It happened in the car, so I jumped out slammed his door and never spoke to him again.

Women. We think we want a gigantic penis until we see one. I was taking the Megabus to see my boyfriend and during the ride, I met a guy. He was traveling to see his significant other. We laughed and talked the entire way to

St. Louis, and eventually we exchanged numbers. We started communicating after that trip, but it was more on a friend level. He traveled back and forth to Chicago, because he was in the "entertaining" business. I later found out "entertaining," meant he was a stripper. I knew I was not going to get serious with him, but I was still curious. So curious that one day I invited him to visit me for the weekend. We hung out downtown, watched movies, and kicked back. Night fell, and it was time for me to put up or shut up. We started, and it was soon time to put the condom on. I had learned my lesson with penectomy, so I turned the lights on immediately.

 The sight that fell before my eyes was unreal. The entertainer was blessed, and I do mean blessed. I had never seen a penis so big! The condom was not fitting on it at all; it looked like a swollen Polish sausage about to burst. I was turned on and scared at the same time. I looked at him said, "Where you think you putting that at"? He just hung his head and start laughing. He explained that he used to trick girls when he was a teenager and only put the head in. I wasn't even that brave. I lied and told him he was moving too fast, we should slow down. I was just scared. He left the next day, and we still talked almost every day. One day I was on my lunch break and who walked up to me? The Entertainer. I was shocked, because I never told him exactly where I worked. I was also in the middle of a conversation with my boyfriend. He said he remembered that I worked across from Union Station. The first pop up was cool. I let that slide, but then he started popping up regularly. One time I and friend were eating lunch and he popped up on us. He gave me his house key and told me to come on home, whatever that meant. He had a live-in girlfriend. I had a boyfriend, and I didn't have any plans on charming his one-eyed snake. I was convinced he was crazy. I cut off all communication with him and never spoke to him again. He did find me on Facebook. We talk…. But that's all.

And finally, I must speak about the guy I call" Mr. Obama" I am only speaking on this situation because young girls have to be mindful about certain admirers. During the time I met Mr. Obama, one of my best friends since kindergarten had been attacked by her boyfriend. The guy beat her with objects, burned her with an iron on both sides of her face, and slit her throat. She survived thank God, but her story taught me. You can't get wined and dined by everyone, especially people you have no real intentions about. I found this out the hard way. I was at Kaplan University about a year when a new class of advisors started. A new guy was added to my team. He was cool. He was from down South, so we clicked. We started talking and going to lunch. We had a lot in common. He wanted to go to Law School and he was interested in Trading like me. I started helping him study for the LSAT, and I hooked him up with another friend that worked with us that was into trading also. I took him around my other friends and we always had a good time. He would buy me $400 shots of liquor and pay my way into everything. I accepted these things under the impression that we were just friends. I was not remotely attracted to him.

One night he took a friend and me out downtown and then to a loft. The loft belonged to a friend of his. He was only house sitting. My friend was in the other room on the phone. I was staring out of the window looking at the view. Suddenly "Mr. Obama" came behind me and wrapped his arms around my waist. He said, "one day we are going to live in a place like this with our kids" I immediately took his hands off me and said, "What"? I know I had been drinking, but I was pretty sure what I had heard. The moment I responded, he kissed me on the lips. I Pulled back, wiped the kiss off and told him I didn't see him like that. I then told my friend we needed to call a cab and get out of there. We left, and he was blowing my phone up. I ignored him. I knew I had to face him at work, so wouldn't deal with him until then. I avoided him for the next week, and Lo and behold he was fired soon after that. I thought I was rid of him then but that was not the case.

Mr. Obama called me day and night, and he was a serial texter. He even called and stalked my friends. He would call and curse me out on one call, and then the next minute he would be crying. He was psychotic. He would call me a ghetto bitch but then say I was his "Michelle Obama." I didn't take him seriously at first until he started sitting outside of my house. He would text and say he was out there, and I didn't believe him. One night I went to look and there he was! I saw him parked on the curb, sitting in his Subaru, and staring at my apartment building. I called the police one him. They said they were unable to do anything to him because he wasn't breaking the law or threatening me. Well, soon enough he started threating me. He started texting me obscene fantasies about me basically being a sex slave and having a million kids. I took those texts to the police got an order of protection. I even sent some guys from the neighborhood after him. They roughed him up, and that still didn't stop him.

Mr. Obama did not sit outside my house anymore, but he kept calling and texting, even after I blocked his number. I would go downtown to shop, and I would be riding down one escalator and he would be riding up the opposite one. He was really starting to freak me out. I decided that I was going to have to kill him. Mr. Obama stopped popping up, calling and texting, for a few weeks, but then the mail started coming. I was getting mail addressed to me and him as Mr. and Mrs. from Harvard Law School. The school was sending me information about admissions and family housing. A representative even called me from the school because my "husband" had given them my information. Mr. Obama's mother even called me, inviting me to come for the holidays. I figured she was just as crazy as her son, so I hung up on her. Mr. Obama soon started texting and calling from other numbers again. I eventually moved from Chicago years later, but he knew where I had moved. He stalked me up until about six years ago. A man is not buying you $400 drinks because wants to be your friend.

I didn't let the situation with "Mr. Obama" scare me. I had a few more work relationships but nothing serious. I was in school and focused during this time. I was working more than forty hours weekly and taking twelve, and sometimes up to eighteen credit hours of school. I was trying to cut my time in half to get into Law School at a certain time. I was taking a lot of "breaks" from my St. Louis boyfriend. He had told me he had a child he supposedly didn't know about. I was focused on me. I didn't feel like I had to settle for a long-distanced relationship with a man who was a father. I had options, safe, uncomplicated options, that didn't require much from me. I needed things to be that way. I made no time for love or feelings. I started having a lot of stress relief, or convenient sex. I scheduled sex. I would send a text telling whoever I was dealing with to come have sex with me. I would be that blunt, and they would oblige. It worked out better that way, considering my lifestyle. I didn't have time for anything more. Eventually, the "convenient" sex and hectic schedule caught up with me.

A Letter to My Unborn Child

Before I knew it, I was a term away from finishing my bachelor's degree in legal studies. I had maintained very good grades, stayed on the dean's list, and been accepted into an academic honors society. I was doing well. Things were stable. My mom had started babysitting, and then somehow managed to become a foster parent. Soon after she wanted to be a licensed daycare provider. To become a licensed daycare provider, she needed a house, she had her eyes set on one. She called me almost every day about this house. My mom did not have good credit or substantial income to buy a house, but she did have the gift of gab. She convinced the man to give her the house with a contract for deed terms. The seller agreed to it, but he had some stipulations. He needed someone to sign, saying that they would be financially responsible if my mom couldn't pay. He also requested a small down payment. I was that someone. My mom knew I would do it for her. The owner of the home contacted me, and we took care of everything. I even took it one step forward and told him I would pay the mortgage. I did it because I knew my mom could not afford the mortgage. She was so convinced that her plan to have the daycare would succeed.

Many people have questioned why I did this and all the other things I did for my mother and she wasn't there for me like she should have been. I felt like I owed her. I felt like all her hardships happened because of me. I always thought to myself, "Well, if she didn't birth me when she was fourteen, she would have had a better life. I tried to give her the life she had lost. I never wanted her to suffer. I did everything in my power to make sure had everything she needed. I was paying utility bills, buying furniture, paying for cars, and paying her mortgage.

I was almost finished with school, and I had added on more responsibility. I was still working at my stressful job, taking eighteen credit hours, and still trying to maintain. I was beyond stressed. I was also planning to relocate for law school. The stress became unbearable. I was arguing with my superiors at work, and I wasn't talking to my friends as much. My Director noticed my attitude one day and suggested I take the day off. I knew then that things were bad. I had never let my stress show at work. I was then diagnosed with Carpal Tunnel and I kept getting sick. Stress affects the immune system and it was doing a number on me. I talked with a co-worker of mine, and she suggested that maybe I could go on FMLA (Family Medical Leave Act) for the stress. I found out it was a possibility. I would have to start seeing a psychiatrist that the company recommended and paid. The psychiatrist would have to recommend the FMLA. I started seeing the psychiatrist and found out so much about myself. I had so many repressed memories. I was in worse shape than I thought. I had so many emotions, inside me that had been just bottled up. My psychiatrist was great. She recommended medicine and healthy ways to get my life back on track. I refused the medicine but took her advice on my health. I was on FMLA, so I had a lot more time for school and myself.

I started eating better, I was working out, and still getting things ready for graduation and relocating. I told my mom I couldn't pay her mortgage anymore. I needed all my money, and I was only getting paid seventy percent of full pay now. She was fine with it, because she was doing ok with her daycare. I was grabbing life by the reins…. or so I thought. Suddenly, my grandpa had to have a serious surgery to avoid a heart attack. I wasn't so sure about leaving Chicago then. I worried about who would care for him when I left? He lived alone, and our family was spread all over Chicago. He and I were really the only ones left on the South Side. We had grown so close, that it was hard imagining not being there with me. My grandpa reassured me that he would be fine. He even told me he was going to propose to one of his many girlfriends and they would live together. I know he only told me that to make me feel better about leaving. I know he could not live with a woman for too long. He was too stuck in his ways and too much of a player to settle down.

Well, things don't always go as planned. One day I was working out before work. I had gone back to work after a month refreshed and ready to get things over with. I felt a dull pain in my side. I then remembered that I had to go get my birth control shot. I had been on the depo shot since I was seventeen. I thought maybe because I was late getting it that my period was returning. I made an appointment to get the shot and took half the day off from work. I was in the waiting room waiting to get called so I could get the shot. The nurse came back, but not to give me the shot. She took me back to the room and said, "Ms. Vaughn, we can't give you the shot today" I looked at her and said, "Why not? "Is it my insurance? She said, "No, you are pregnant" My mouth dropped open. I asked her, "how did that happen? She replied, "I don't know I wasn't there". I had been coming to this very same clinic since I was seventeen years old visiting Chicago. I had been on the shot for almost ten years, had always used protection, and hadn't had any accidents. I could not be pregnant. I took the card she gave me with the number of weeks I was and left. I took the bus home and dismissed what she said.

A few days later I told my friend at work what the nurse had said. I still did not believe her. She laughed so hard and asked why didn't I believe the nurse? I told her because I had been on the shot and been using protection. I could not be pregnant. My friend said that she was going to bring some pregnancy tests over after work just to make sure. She brought three pregnancy tests and they all said positive. I still wasn't convinced. It had to be a mistake. Louis still worked at the hospital so, I called her and told her I was going to work with her the next day. I wanted to confirm the pregnancy. I was still in denial.

I could not be pregnant. I went to work with Lois the next day and sure enough the results were that I was pregnant. I finally let it sink in. I was devastated. I had already started packing my house. I had already informed my job I was resigning, and what about law school?

Aside, from that, I hadn't even thought once about the father. He was one of the guys I had convenient sex with. We weren't exclusive. It was just a "Hey come over have sex with me and leave because I have studying to do and work in the morning. I told him about my pregnancy, he wasn't too thrilled, but he was supportive. We were both about to start new journeys in our lives and having a baby was not ideal for either one of us. I then decided I would have an abortion. He would pay for it and take me to the clinic. It was settled. It wasn't settled, because in my heart of hearts I knew it was wrong. If I really wanted to have an abortion, I wouldn't have told anyone. I told my cousin, Arnetta, at the time she was the only one I could trust with the information. She told me I shouldn't do it, but the decision was up to me. We then joked that either way I wouldn't be able to drink on our trip to New York. I wouldn't be able to drink because of the abortion or because of the pregnancy I didn't know what to do. I was almost at the finish line, and here I was pregnant. I thought about it a few more days and after talking to my aunt. She told me I was a murderer of my own flesh and that I was shedding innocent blood. I decided to keep the baby. I was an adult, about to earn a second degree, and very capable of caring for a child. I did not have a legitimate reason to have an abortion. The only reasons were that the timing was all wrong, and I didn't have a relationship with the father. At first the father was not happy that I had changed my mind, but he quickly came around. My own conception was a secret. My birth was a surprise. My life was a combination of both.

I still wanted to attend law school. I had already given up everything. I figured things could still go as planned, but I was wrong about that. The father was very upset that I was leaving town with his unborn child. He felt like all my decisions should have been discussed with him. I was not having that. I cursed him out several time. I even slapped him in the face because I started to feel like I had been set up. I couldn't stand him anymore. I went right along with my plans, and before I knew it, my mom and best friend were in town for my graduation. I had finally made it, but my entire plan was unraveling by the minute. I was horrible. I was irritated and annoyed by everything. I was graduating, I was still packing to leave, and I was almost two months pregnant. Everything that I had been through and worked for had come down to this moment. I had earned my bachelor's degree so I could go to Law School. The thought of that possibly not happening made me sick to my stomach. I walked across the stage in August 2010 with honors. I still had to prepare to move six hours away.

My mom took the train up to Chicago, to help me move and drive the U-Haul back. (I still didn't have a license.) My uncle, mom, and cousins helped me move. We were getting along well; we were almost out of Chicago and boom! We had a wreck. My mom was not paying attention, took a wrong turn, and caused a lady in a van to hit us. The entire trip was awful. We argued the entire time, and I was so uncomfortable. We were going to Energy, Illinois, where I would be living, and we could not get there faster. I chose to live there because it was closer to Carbondale and cheaper. One of my old friends from grade school lived in Energy, and I had relatives in Carbondale, so I wouldn't be completely by myself. My mom also lived an hour away. Energy was a small, quiet town, exactly what I needed. We finally made it, but we went to Carbondale instead, because we kept getting lost. We stayed at my cousin's house and tried again the next day. We finally found my apartment and moved my stuff in.

My first night alone in my new apartment felt strange. It was so quiet, and Lois wasn't next door or across the way. Grandpa was not a bus ride away. I didn't have a cab to call and take me anywhere. I didn't have any of the restaurants I loved. I laid there thinking, "What have I gotten myself into?

Moving to the middle of nowhere pregnant." I wanted to turn around and go back to Chicago. Energy didn't have any public transportation system. My entire life in Chicago revolved around public transportation. Now, I was here stuck, without a license or a car. I would have to be dependent on someone, and that was not cool with me. I had relocation remorse. The car situation was supposed to be settled before I moved. My mom had agreed that I could buy her car for $3,000, because she was going to get a new one. I sent her the money before I moved, but she never mentioned the car again. I decided I would give it awhile, since I didn't have my license. My mama refused to give me the car. She took my money with no intentions on giving me the car. I asked, and asked, and finally she said that the money was spent on my graduation party. The party was nice, but surely did not cost $3000. She had gotten me again.

I got settled in and got straight to work. The first line of business was to find a doctor. It wasn't hard to find a doctor; the town was small and there wasn't many to choose from. I had everything set up in Energy. Then, I had to take care of school. I had signed up for a law school Prep class. I went to the university for the class and found out that I could start law school the following semester, but they didn't have classes on weekends or evening classes. Also, if I took time off to give birth, I would have to start over. These stipulations were not conducive to my current circumstances. I hadn't planned on working. I had money saved up to at least get through the first year or two of law school. I was pregnant now, so I had to work. I would need childcare. The money I had saved would not be enough to care for a child. I also had to figure out what I was going to do about transportation. My dreams were being crushed. I did not know what to do next. I only gave up everything and moved to the middle of nowhere to attend law school, but now that was in jeopardy.

I had to find work. I had a nice amount of money saved, but I knew it could go fast, especially with nothing coming in. I searched for jobs and found nothing. It was Chicago all over again. The positions that I knew that I was qualified for and had the education for, were not offered. The jobs I worked in Chicago when I only had an associate's degree now required a master's degree. I was so shocked. The jobs were paying half of what I had made before but required advanced degrees. I was fed up and getting further along with my pregnancy.

I was also going through culture shock. I went from living in a city surrounded by people that looked like me, to living in the middle of nowhere and sticking out like a sore thumb. Everyone gave me the side-eye everywhere I went. I was this young, pregnant girl, wearing an afro or natural hairstyle most of the time. Every store, restaurant, and business was predominately white. Nothing was black owned. I was so used to Chicago, seeing so many white people all the time was strange to me. Chicago wasn't the best, but you could feel the people's pride, no matter how much or little they had. I knew in my heart that I had made a mistake. While my folks were happy, that I was close to home again, I stayed up all night longing for my one-bedroom apartment in Englewood. Everything that I did to get out, I wanted to return to once I left. I missed my friends. I missed my privacy. I wasn't used to my people just stopping by my house and knowing my every move. My mom and grandmother smothered me. I couldn't do anything without them knowing about it. I couldn't go anywhere without a family member. I had done what I wanted when I wanted for so long, that the new circumstances were too much for me.

Finally, I found out about a work-from-home job from a friend in Chicago. I started working from home doing technical support for Microsoft. It was the perfect job for me. I sat down the entire time, and I didn't have to worry about getting back and forth to work. I was really blessed to have that job, but I wasn't content with just working. I felt like something was missing. So, I enrolled in the master's program at the Kaplan University. My experience the last five years was in Higher Education, but my degree was in Legal Studies. I figured my Master's should be in Higher Education since that is what my experience was in. I enrolled, and I was back to working and going to school, in my comfort zone. I was getting bigger and bigger, and the weather was getting colder and colder. I still missed Chicago and my grandpa. One day I just bought a ticket for the three-a.m. train Chicago. I only told my cousin, who took me to the train. I had lunch with my child's father to discuss some things. I hung out with Lois and watched the Super Bowl in a hotel downtown. My mom and grandma were furious that I had just left without telling anyone. I was now 8 months pregnant and not supposed to be riding on a train that long. I needed the break. I went out to eat with my grandpa and almost stayed. I wasn't going to go back to Energy, but I knew I had to return.

I kept having issues with low blood pressure. Also, my baby was so big that my doctor was concerned that I would contract stationary diabetes. He suggested that my labor be induced. I agreed, but I did not want it to be so early. He said that I could possibly go until a week before my due date. I was disappointed that I wouldn't get to experience the excitement of not knowing when labor came or my water breaking. I knew what I had to do for health reasons though. My induce date was March 3, 2011. I went to Red Lobsters, ate an entire ultimate feast, and checked into the hospital. My mom was with me the entire time, and two cousins came later that evening. I remained in labor, and the doctor thought I wouldn't have the baby for another day or two. The next day he asked if I wanted him to break my water, and I said yes. I was contracting and in pain. He broke my water, and then said he was going to get a haircut and take his wife out. He did not get down the hall too far, before began yelling "Get him back" 'This baby is coming" Everyone kept saying no, that it just like it. When the nurse checked, I was nine-and-a- half centimeters. It was pushing time! The deal was this: I was only getting one chance to push the baby out or I would have to get a c-section. I didn't want this, so I gave it four big pushes, and my ten-pound baby boy was born. March 4th, 2011, Adam Greyson Kirkwood was born. It was surreal., I had really had a baby. I couldn't believe it. The funny thing is that even before the birth or ultrasound, I knew I was having a boy. My grandma has already bought boy clothes. My mother kept saying it would be a boy, I believed her too. My grandma used to always say "You aren't blessed until you have a child, and you are really blessed if you have a boy". She was partial to boys. I was blessed. Adam is my blessing.

Motherhood was something that required adjustment. I was twenty-five years old; I had had a lot of time to myself before Adam's birth. I was still working from home, so my mom kept him on the days that I worked and brought him home to me on my off days. I worked from home until Adam was two months. The program I was working for ended. I was still able to stay home because of the money I had saved and the unemployment I was receiving. I can honestly say I had it easy. I did not have to worry about finances or childcare. Our life was good but simple. It became too mundane. I was getting bored and weary. I still longed for Chicago. My cousin went to Chicago a lot, and Adam and I tagged along every chance that we could. Adam was a good baby; he didn't whine or cry all the time. He was independent early on. I was still in school for my Master's, so I had lots of work to do. Adam would sit quietly or in his bouncer and playpen and entertain himself while I typed thirty-page papers. He started babbling early on. He did well at all of his doctor's appointments. He was a happy, healthy baby. He was diagnosed with asthma and had two febrile seizures, but for the most part he did not have any major medical issues. Things were "good" until they weren't.

Adam had turned a year old when I returned to work. I was faced with the same issues. Overqualified for most jobs or not able to work the schedule. I applied at a health-insurance company. Everyone swore it was the best job to have in the area. The pay was good. They had great benefits, great hours, and weekends off. I needed this job. I got the job, but I had to train for a month and could not miss any days. However, as soon as I started the job, things started unraveling. I enrolled Adam in a nearby daycare, but he kept getting sick. He kept having ear infections and fevers. I had to find sitters when he could not go to daycare, and I didn't know a too many people in the area. My mother lived an hour away and was running her own daycare. I wanted to quit my job. I wanted my baby to just stay home with me like we before. I couldn't do that anymore. My money was running out. I had bills that needed to be paid. I couldn't quit. I didn't want to get fired. Aside from Adam getting sick all the time, other kids kept biting and being aggressive with him. I eventually got tired of yelling at the daycare workers and found another daycare center. The daycare center I found was smaller, more expensive, but right in town. I could drop Adam off and head straight to work. The new daycare was much better. Adam did not get as sick as much, and finally we got into a groove. I would drop him off, go to work until five, pick him up, then come home and do homework. This was how it went up until Adam was about eighteen months. If hindsight were 20/20, I would have cherished this calm. I would have relished in the peace and tranquility, But I didn't. I was always worried, trying to stay two steps ahead and waiting on the other shoe to drop. Well, it did. I'm not sure if I willed the next events in my life from all the expecting and worrying, but I sure felt like I did. The other shoe dropped like bombs on Pearl Harbor.

Shed So Many Tears

Adam was almost eighteen months when the daycare owner said she needed to speak to me about something important. She expressed her concern that Adam may be deaf. She explained that Adam no longer responded to the other children or gave them eye contact. I told her I had noticed the same thing. I had watched him with the other children at daycare and saw how they were progressing faster. I watched how he played *around* children but not *with* them. I noticed at home how he didn't respond to the vacuum cleaner like a child would normally. I noticed how he only seemed to hear Mickey Mouse and rocked back and forth while watching it. I had noticed and watched it all. I never thought he was deaf. I just thought he was progressing slowly.

The teacher's observation did send off alarms for me. What if he did go deaf? What if I waited too late to do anything about it? How could I have not had picked up on it? I asked myself these questions repeatedly. I did not have time to sit and think about the what ifs. I then contacted his primary doctor, and she did a hearing test. Adam's doctor said his hearing was fine, I was not convinced. I asked for a referral for an ear, nose, and throat doctor. (ENT) I received the referral, but my health insurance would not pay for the additional hearing tests. I paid $250 for the first hearing test. The ENT said Adam could hear, but I was not convinced. I asked him to do another one because Adam was not cooperative during the first one. I wanted to make sure. The ENT performed a second hearing test, the results were the same. Adam could hear. I still was not convinced. The ENT told me about a test that would require Adam to be put to sleep so they could conduct a test on his brain to test his hearing. I told him to do it. The result was the same. Adam could hear. The ENT told me maybe something else was going on mentally. I asked him what he meant by "mentally" The ENT said maybe something is not connecting for Adam. He said maybe Adam couldn't understand what he was hearing. The ENT mentioned the word Autism. I had never thought about Autism. I had heard it a few times but never read about it. I asked the ENT what I needed to do to find out if Adam was autistic. He told me to get a referral from Adam's primary doctor so a specialist could test and diagnose him.

I contacted Adam's doctor right away. She was against it from the start. She told me she was not the least bit worried about Adam. He was healthy and his Apgar was good. (An APGAR is an appearance, pulse, grimace, activity, and respiration test given to newborns right after birth.) She said some children just progress slower than others. She told me she had two boys on the autism spectrum, so she knew Autism. She was certain that Adam was not autistic. I still did not feel better. I went home and started researching Autism. I found these assessment tools online that tell you if your child needed to be tested. The more I read and completed the tests, the more I felt like I was reading my own story. The signs were all pointing to Autism. The parents I read about had been taken on the same journey. I had answered yes to almost every question on the assessments and tests. I knew in my heart that, more than likely, Adam was autistic. I went back to his primary doctor, but she refused to give me a referral to a specialist. She did not think it was necessary, and they only diagnosed children three and up with Autism. Adam was not two yet. I was at a crossroads. I needed to get Adam tested, but my insurance would not pay without the referral and they also informed me that Adam was not old enough.

I researched and researched. I became more adamant that Adam needed to be tested for Autism. Then, one day, I thought about the ENT. He was the first person to mention that maybe something else was going on with Adam, so maybe he could give me the referral. My insurance said I needed a referral. Adam's primary doctor kept refusing. I talked to an insurance rep. She informed me that I could use the referral from the ENT, but everything after the diagnosis would be my responsibility. I contacted the ENT immediately, and he gave me the referral. We finally got an appointment to see a doctor at Cardinal Glennon Children's Medical Center. I had overcome one obstacle, but I had plenty more to go. It was explained to me that after the diagnosis, Adam would need therapy, therapies that the state usually would pay for. I would not be able to receive any assistance from the state until Adam was three. I was not going to wait that long, as Adam just made two years old. I started going over all my finances and credit-card limits. I knew that I was going to exhaust every dime I had to make sure Adam received whatever he needed. I had made a lot of sacrifices for myself and others, so there was no doubt that I was going to go head-to-head with Autism full force. I was prepared for anything, at least I thought I was prepared.

In the meantime, I was still working and completing my Master's. The appointment was so far away that I sometimes forgot about it. I tried to continue on with my life just as I had before, but, It was hard. My thoughts consumed me. It seemed like Adam started showing more and more signs of Autism as time went by. I was on edge and trying to keep it all together. I did not involve anyone else. I wanted to be sure it was Autism. I had so many questions that I needed answered before I could answer anyone else's questions. My family accused me of being embarrassed, or not wanting to be knocked off of my "high horse," I just did not know enough to discuss it. I needed to get a handle on things before bringing everyone else in. The only people I told were my grandparents, my grandfather in Chicago, and my grandmother in Southern Illinois. I was closer to them than anyone. I did not and could not keep anything from them. Every step of the way they reassured me that Adam was fine and was going to always be fine. For the first time in my life, I had doubts about what they were saying. I thought my grandparents hung the moon and stars, but I knew they were still old-fashioned. My grandparents did not believe in taking everything the doctor said as facts. I knew that they could not even begin to understand what I was really dealing with. Telling me to just pray, or that, "Wasn't nothing wrong with Adam" didn't help me at all. I waited on the appointment. My mother was putting on events for the community. My grandmother had separated from her husband and moved into her own place, and my grandfather had another surgery. Life and its changes continued.

April 6, 2013 was the day of my mother's walk for people that we have lost to violence. The day before I had found out that one of my classmates had been killed. I felt bad the entire day. I almost did not go to the town my grandmother and mother lived in to attend the walk. I had to, though, because I had to give my grandmother her separation papers that she had asked me to draw up. So, I went where they lived. My grandmother and mother lived on the same street, one house away from each other. I pulled into my mother's driveway and noticed that my grandmother's car was there, I figured I would go see her after I helped my mom. As soon as we got of the car, Adam ran to my grandmother's house. My mother told him she was not there; she had gone out to eat with a friend. I told her it was strange that my grandmother hadn't checked her mail. We did not focus on it too much, as we had the walk to prepare for. Family members came back and forth to my mother's house bringing food and things for the event. Occasionally, someone would ask where my grandmother was, and someone would say she was here or there. I had to make a run to the store to grab a t-shirt for one of my younger cousins, so I left my mom's house. Upon returning to the house, I saw police, an ambulance and a crowd. My initial thought was that someone had been in a car accident. My mom had several cars in front of her house, and so did my grandmother. As I drove closer to the house, I heard a male cousin scream on his phone, "My granny is gone" (I have had to take a pause while writing this. It still takes my breath away when those words replay in my head.) Those were the worst words I've heard in my life. I blacked out and lost control of my car. A family member helped stopped my car and grabbed Adam and my cousin out of the car. I got out and ran to my grandmother's house. The scene I walked upon is forever etched in my brain. My mother was screaming at the top of her lungs. Paramedics were everywhere, and my grandmother was on the floor in her nightgown. Her nightgown was going up and down as they performed CPR on her. I couldn't take it. I ran back out of the door. The paramedics put my grandmother in the ambulance. I grabbed a paramedic and said, "Please save my granny." He just walked off. A friend of the family walked up to me and another cousin of mine and said, "We have pulse" she might be ok.

We drove behind the ambulance still with hope that she would be ok. We got to the hospital, and I burst through doors asking her whereabouts'. To this day I don't remember who said, "She is gone." but I passed out after hearing those words. My mother said someone had to catch Adam. When I came to, I still couldn't wrap my mind around the fact that we were there, but my grandmother was gone. The hospital scene was a circus. People were crying, cursing, and almost fighting. Everyone had lost control. I had to see her to feel like it was real. Once I did, left the hospital. She was gone. She had died during the night asleep in her chair from a heart attack. The whole time we were convinced she was somewhere; she was next door dead. If my cousin hadn't become worried and insisted one of my aunts open the door, who knows when she would have been found. She used to always say "I have to make sure I'm clean and put a little eyeliner on because if something happens to me, it's only going to take my kids five minutes to find me". In reality, it took us much longer. We were so busy getting ready for the event and running around that it never crossed our minds that anything could be wrong. To our knowledge she was not sick, so her death was truly unexpected.

Losing my grandmother meant something different to us. To me, it was the end of the world, at least it felt that way. I had lived with my grandmother; she had practically raised me. I talked to her every day. She knew me better than anyone. I used to get home from school or work late coming off of the train or bus, and she would stay on the phone with me until she heard me close the gate to my apartment building. She prayed for me daily. She was my best friend, confidant, and protector. She was one of the two people that knew what I was going through with Adam. I had lost so many things in losing her. I was so angry. I asked God why; "Why did you have to take her so soon? What am I supposed to do now? I needed her more than ever at this time, and now she was gone. I didn't sleep or eat for days leading up to the funeral. I could only manage what I had to do for Adam. The entire family started falling apart. There were too many emotions, and no one knew what to do with them. My grandfather and uncles took me to the funeral, but I couldn't sit for the entire service. I couldn't go to the burial site either. I refused to look down in the casket at her, and I couldn't handle seeing her being lowered the ground. The end of my grandmother's life was the beginning of a new life for me. I had been transformed. I did not think, act, or feel the same. Life was different. About to get to more interesting.

Two months later, June 4th, 2013 Adam was diagnosed with Autism. The doctor told me I would never hear Adam's voice again. He said Adam could be mentally retarded. He told me Adam would be considered "special needs." He would be in special classes and need therapy. I heard him, but for some reason it didn't devastate me. I had a sudden sense of reassurance and calm. I felt like Adam would be ok, as my grandmother's words kept playing in my head. I did not cry that day in the doctor's office. I started on the next steps. I set up therapy for late evenings and paid for them myself. For months I would go to work, come home, and then Adam would have therapy. Then I would stay up and do homework. I went through this while beating myself up. I wondered what I'd done for this have happened. I felt like God was punishing me by taking my grandmother and with my son having this disability. I felt like the things that I'd done in my past caused this. I was getting my payback. I had possibly taken two lives and contributed to destroying other lives. This was my karma. One day it became too much. I found myself balled up on the floor in my bathroom, begging and crying out for my grandmother to help heal my baby. I told her since she was up there with God to ask him to heal Adam. I made a deal that day. I told God if he gave me just a little extra strength to get through the grief and Adam's diagnosis that I would only us it for good. I wouldn't blame anyone, sue doctors, be angry, or feel sorry for myself or Adam. Adam is eight years old now and has a YouTube channel. I believe God kept his end of the deal, and so did I.

Only God Can Judge Me

There is no blueprint for life. You will go through things that you could never imagine and still come out on the other end. Life is about choices; you will make good ones and bad ones. The key to surviving is being true to yourself. Be honest and accept what you put out will come back. I've never blamed anyone for anything. I have expected and accepted karma if I put something bad out into the universe. The saying is, "You gone bow now or you gone bow later, but you gone bow," I have bowed many times, but I have also gotten back up. Life has taught me how to keep going. When the odds are against you, you are going to fight or flee. I'm a fighter, not a statistic, a drug dealer, a whore, or a gold digger, just a fighter. Life's events made me who I am today. All these events made me able to exert strength, passion and dedication to my son's wellbeing and survival.

The thing about these situations, was that I didn't feel bad. I didn't care about being involved with drugs, I had to survive. I didn't care about stabbing and possibly shooting anyone. In my mind, it was them or me, I chose me. I didn't know if they were going to rape, beat, or kill me. The worst thing about this state of mind was that I knew if I had to, I would do it again, without hesitation. Mix seeing violence and abuse at a young age, always having to be on guard, and being displaced on the regular with going through what I went through in the first three years in Chicago and you can say I was troubled. I had never trusted anyone, and those last three years only made that worse. I was always private and cautious, but now I had legitimate reasons to be. The worst thing was that I didn't have a conscience. I tell people all the time, "The more a person gets away with, the more chances they will take; they will feel "empowered." I didn't think I was untouchable, but I knew I was a force to be reckoned with. I had survived so much that I was prepared for anything or anyone that got in my way. I always say I was country-made but city-raised.

I knew better than to be involved with drugs, and stabbing and shooting people, I was not raised that way. I knew right from wrong. I knew that one day it would all come back on me. I just didn't care. It started with me only being concerned with my plan to finish school. Then it was I needed money to stay afloat. Then I had to take care of my mama. I kept adding on excuses when the truth was this; I loved money and lots of it. I loved spending it too. The crazy thing is that even when I was out doing wrong, I always prayed for my safety and for the Lord to watch over me. I can't say that I had faith though; I was too impatient for that. I wasn't in the "wait for the Lord he will work it out" mind frame. I felt like it was all on me. I had to take care of me. Nobody else was going to come through for me like I would come through for myself. In my eyes I had been in hell since I was child, and God hadn't magically turned things around, so he sure wasn't going to pop up now.

I was young and immature. I knew God, but I didn't believe in God's power. I had no idea how much God loved me or that I only needed to rely on him. I took being self-sufficient to another level. I even thought I was doing the right things, because it was all to reach positive goals that I had set. I thought I had it all figured out. I was so wrong, and God showed me. The miracles that God worked in my life no one could manage but him. No amount of money or number of degrees could measure up to his grace and mercy. I will never be anything without God. There is no beating the odds without him. I was never against the odds alone. I was so foolish to think that. He was there the entire time. I just did not accept it. His judgement is the only one I am concerned about. He made me, and he molded me.

Made in the USA
Columbia, SC
28 February 2020